A Beginner's Guide to Informatics and Artificial
Intelligence

Wei Weng

A Beginner's Guide to Informatics and Artificial Intelligence

A Short Course Towards Practical Problem Solving

 Springer

Wei Weng
Institute of Liberal Arts and Science
Kanazawa University
Kanazawa, Ishikawa, Japan

ISBN 978-981-97-1476-6   ISBN 978-981-97-1477-3   (eBook)
https://doi.org/10.1007/978-981-97-1477-3

This Springer imprint is published by the registered company Springer Nature Singapore Pte Ltd.
The registered company address is: 152 Beach Road, #21-01/04 Gateway East, Singapore 189721,
Singapore

Paper in this product is recyclable.

Preface

Background and Purpose

In today's technology-driven world, computer science, artificial intelligence (AI), and data science have emerged as foundational pillars that shape our digital landscape. As these fields continue to evolve and weave themselves into every aspect of our life, it is becoming increasingly essential for individuals from all walks of life to gain a solid understanding of their fundamentals.

The purpose of this book is to unlock the seemingly mysterious domains of computer science, AI, and data science, particularly for those who are taking their first steps into this realm. While these domains might appear intimidating at first glance, they possess an inherent beauty and logic that can be understood by anyone with the right guidance.

We created this book to enable swift transformation from a novice to a problem solver by providing a seamless learning experience from introducing basic concepts to engaging learners in practical problem-solving exercises. This carefully selected and designed course spanning seven to nine classes ensures that busy individuals can grasp the essentials swiftly and efficiently.

Whether your aim is to pursue a career in technology, undertake research projects, or simply understand the workings of the digital age, this book lays a sturdy foundation upon which you can build. As you progress in your studies and pursuit, we hope that the knowledge and skills gained from this book will enable you to contribute to the future of the exciting discipline of information science and AI.

Topics and Organization of Contents

This book covers a wide range of topics including computer, flowchart, time complexity, mathematical modeling, genetic algorithm, machine learning, network, database, and information security.

The organization of contents is as follows. We start from the underlying mechanisms of computers, how they process and store information, and the fundamental principles of logic operations (Chap. 1). This lays the groundwork for the subsequent exploration of problem solving and algorithmic thinking. We then introduce flowchart (Chap. 2), a commonly used method to show technical processes such as programs and algorithms. By highlighting the relations between programs, flowcharts, and time complexity, we move to computation efficiency (Chap. 3), which underlies the importance of applying AI algorithms.

Then we guide learners to use AI algorithms for problem solving by showing how to build models and encode solutions (Chap. 4) and apply genetic algorithm as an example (Chap. 5). Through clear explanations, vivid examples, and illustrative flowcharts, we ensure that each step is not only understood but also embraced. After that, we introduce machine learning (Chap. 6), another popular AI branch where we focus on neural network. We show how a neuron can produce various outcomes according to need by giving step-to-step examples.

After our journey in the AI realm, we introduce network (Chap. 7), database (Chap. 8), and information security (Chap. 9) by showing the backbones of these modern technologies.

For each topic, we provide questions to activate learners' thinking and hands-on exercises for learners to gain practical experience. We give instructions and guidance for the exercises. Through guided problem-solving, we empower learners to think systematically and algorithmically, raising their ability in creation and coping with difficulties.

Features of this Book

1. Beginner-friendly: this book is tailored specifically for beginners in informatics and AI, making it accessible to individuals with no prior technical background.
2. Concise and condensed: this book is designed for an accelerated curriculum where time is limited but the goal is to transform beginners to part of the intelligent future. We have carefully crafted the content to be concise and condensed without compromising on clarity or depth of the material, ensuring that learners will receive a well-rounded education that can serve as a strong foundation for their future pursuits.
3. Integration of information science and AI: this book covers a wide range of topics from basic computer concepts to advanced AI techniques. By combining these two disciplines, we aim to provide learners with a holistic understanding of how computers, data, and algorithms are interconnected to shape our modern world. The topics are basically independent, but each chapter is built upon the previous ones to gradually expand learners' knowledge and problem-solving abilities.
4. Step-by-step guidance: each chapter is enriched with detailed calculation procedures and problem-solving examples that illustrate the concepts discussed,

ensuring that learners can witness how to apply what they learn in the classroom to research and practical applications.

5. Practical hands-on exercises: each chapter is accompanied by questions and exercises. By engaging with real-world scenarios, learners will not only comprehend the theories but also develop the skills to tackle challenges they might encounter in the field.

6. Immediate guidance: hint for questions and detailed guidance for exercises are given immediately after each problem, aiding learners in their problem-solving process. Solutions to exercises are provided in Chap. 10 along with explanations.

7. Preparation for the future: this book fosters an environment where complex concepts are made accessible, curiosity is nurtured, and creation is welcome. With this book in hand, learners will not only understand the world of computer science, AI, and data science but also be able to navigate more ambitious journey in their future pursuits.

How to Use this Book

This book can be used for a course spanning seven to nine 90-min classes. In the case of seven classes, Chaps. 2 and 3, and Chaps. 8 and 9 can be combined into one class, respectively.

For each class, we recommend that the instructor explains the content while asking the listed questions first, then guides the learners as they work on the exercises, and finally presents the solutions. The questions and exercise problems without an asterisk (*) symbol are intended to be completed in class, while those marked with an asterisk (*) can be assigned as homework or left for learners who are interested to work on independently.

For self-learners, we recommend that you read the content and think about the questions first, then work on the exercise problems without an asterisk (*) symbol before checking the solutions in Chap. 10. If you are interested in enhancing your ability, further work on the exercise problems with an asterisk (*) and check their solutions.

To enhance your understanding and improve your learning experience, lecture videos for this book will soon be available in Springer Nature Video, named "Informatics and Artificial Intelligence for Beginners I and II". You may watch the videos at your convenience.

Acknowledgements

We extend our heartfelt gratitude to all the colleagues who have played a role in shaping this book. This textbook was created in 2018 and has been refined over five years through extensive use and feedback from more than 5000 students. The valuable input from faculty, editor, and students has greatly contributed to the improvement of this book and the learning experience.

Finally, we would like to express our sincere appreciation to you, the reader, for embarking on this learning journey with us. We believe that this book will empower you to navigate and pursue further in the fantastic fields of informatics and AI. Best wishes for a rewarding and fulfilling learning experience!

Kanazawa, Japan   Wei Weng
January 2024

Contents

List of Figures

List of Tables

Chapter 1
Computer

1.1 What is a Computer

In the seventeenth century, the term "computer" described a man whose job was calculation, whereas the term "computress" was used to refer to a woman in the same role. Over time, "computer" also evolved to denote a device designed for performing calculations.

Computers can be classified into two categories based on how they process information: analog computers and digital computers. Analog computers process information using continuous analog quantities, whereas digital computers process information using discrete digits. Further details will be provided in the following.

There are two types of signals: analog signal and digital signal. Analog signals represent continuous quantities. For example, temperature and voltage are considered analog signals because they are continuous quantities. Analog displays represent these continuous values such as by using the position of a needle (Fig. 1.1).

In contrast, digital signals represent discrete values. A digital display conveys information such as temperature and voltage using numerical representations. The display is limited to showing values within the range of its available digits. For example, in Fig. 1.2, the display reads "12,345.6". In this context, "discrete values" means that values between 12,345.5 and 12,345.6 cannot be displayed. Additionally, "within the range of its available digits" means that values with more than two decimal places, such as "12,345.67", cannot be displayed.

In mathematics, real numbers are analog quantities because they represent continuous values without interruption. In contrast, integers are digital quantities because they are discrete values such as 0, 1, and 2.

Computers can also be classified as either mechanical or electronic, depending on the components used in their construction. Early analog computers are built using mechanical components like gears and levers, making them mechanical computers. In contrast, modern digital computers are built using electronic components, such as transistors and integrated circuits, making them electronic computers. Today the

W. Weng, *A Beginner's Guide to Informatics and Artificial Intelligence*,
https://doi.org/10.1007/978-981-97-1477-3_1

Fig. 1.1 An example of
analog display

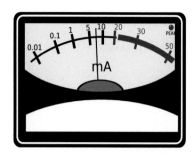

Fig. 1.2 An example of
digital display

overwhelming majority of computers are electronic digital computers, so the term
"computer" hereinafter refers to electronic digital computers.

1.2 Program and Programming

A program (also called code) is a human-written modifiable calculation procedure. It
consists of multiple "instructions", often guiding the execution of elementary operations such as "retrieve data from storage" and "add these numbers". For example,
Fig. 1.3 is a Java program that outputs the sum of two integers a and b, being 5 and
3, respectively.

```
public static void main (String argv[]) {
        int a = 5;
        int b = 3;
        System.out.println(a+b);
}
```

Fig. 1.3 An example of a Java program

The main body of a program is typically written in English, using alphabets, numbers, and symbols including commas and line breaks. This practice can be attributed to historical factors, such as the initial limitation to English of early computers, the prevalent use of English within the field of computer science, and the necessity for a standardized and universally comprehensible language to facilitate global code collaboration and sharing.

Writing a program is called programming. The formal language for writing programs is called a programming language. There are many programming languages such as Python, Java, C++, and JavaScript. These popular and widely used programming languages all employ English-based syntax and keywords, and this is one of the reasons why English is prevalent in programming.

1.3 Distinguishing Characteristic of a Computer

The key difference between a "computer" and a "calculator" is that a computer can automatically execute calculations based on a program, whereas a calculator requires manual operation. Hence, a computer is a programmable electronic digital computing device.

A computer can perform various calculations automatically if the program is changed. In contrast, a basic calculator, like a pocket calculator, relies on human operation. Complex calculations with a calculator demand manual operation for each step.

• Questions

1. Is a smartphone a computer?

    Hint: consider whether a smartphone has the same characteristic as that of a computer.

1.4 Composition of a Computer

The basic components of a computer (Fig. 1.4) are.

- the computing and control unit,
- the storage unit,
- the input/output (I/O) unit,

Fig. 1.4 Composition of a
computer

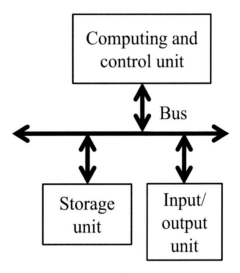

and the "buses" that connect these units [1]. The computing and control unit performs calculations and controls the entire computer. The storage unit stores programs that define computational procedures and the data to be processed. The input/output unit obtains information from the outside and presents calculation results.

The computing and control unit is also called the central processing unit (CPU). In modern computers, the CPU is often combined with integrated circuits (ICs), which include many electronic logic gates. An electronic logic gate has an elementary computational function. More details of logic gates will be given in Sect. 1.7.

The storage unit has many blocks for storing programs and data. The location is indicated by a serial number (usually an integer) called address. The minimum size of storage is called a "bit", which stores only one "0" or "1". A group of eight bits is called a "byte". Addresses are often assigned in byte units.

The input unit receives information from a human. There are many input devices such as keyboards, mice, styluses, handwriting panels, microphones, and cameras. The output unit delivers information to a human. Output devices include displays, printers, speakers, and earphones.

1.5 Hardware and Software of a Computer

Originally, the term "hardware" referred to machinery or devices made of physical materials, often including iron components. In contrast, "software" is a term used to distinguish the non-physical aspects of computing. In the context of a computer, "hardware" refers to its physical components (Fig. 1.5a), whereas "software" refers to the computational procedures and programs that enable its functionality (Fig. 1.5b). Hence, in a computer, hardware operates according to software [2].

1. Let X be 10
2. Let Y be 0
3. Update Y to be X + Y
4. Update X to be X-1
5. Return to 3 if X > 0

(a) Example of hardware   (b) Example of software

Fig. 1.5 Examples of hardware and software in a computer

A computer executes a program in the following procedure:

1. Retrieve instructions from the storage unit.
2. Translate the instructions into machine-readable code.
3. Prepare necessary data.
4. Perform calculation.
5. Store or output the calculation results.
6. Repeat the above steps.

1.6 Representation of Information Inside a Computer

A computer processes all information as digital quantities, represented by combinations of "0" and "1" known as bits. A computer system where the high voltage (or large current) state represents "1" and the low voltage (or small current) state represents "0" is called a "positive logic" system. In contrast, a system where the low voltage state represents "1" and the high voltage state represents "0" is called a "negative logic" system [2]. Which type of system to use should be determined according to need.

A number inside a computer is represented by its binary value, consisting of "0" and "1".

A character is represented by a numerical value corresponding to the character in the character code used. A character code is a correspondence table linking characters and their corresponding numerical values. There are many types of character codes. The American Standard Code for Information Interchange (ASCII) has been in use since the mid-twentieth century. It uses seven bits to represent an uppercase or lowercase English alphabet, an Arabic number (0–9), a symbol, and a control character such as a line break. For example, the number "0" is expressed by binary 0,110,000 (= decimal 48), and the uppercase letter "A" is expressed by binary 1,000,001 (= decimal 65).

A kanji character in languages such as Japanese cannot be represented by only 1 byte (8 bits), so a kanji is represented by two or more bytes. There are several

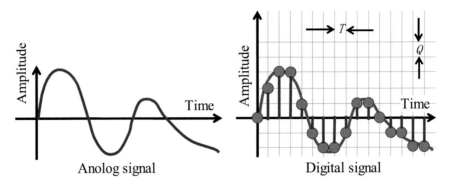

Fig. 1.6 An example of converting an analog signal to a digital signal

character codes associating Japanese characters with numbers such as JIS, Shift-JIS, and EUC-JP. In recent years, Unicode has gained increasing prominence. It aims to handle all the characters in the world, including emoji that is often used in mobile messages [2].

Audio and images are converted to digital numbers before being processed. Sound is change in air pressure over time. Since air pressure and time are both continuous quantities, sound is an analog quantity. To be processed inside a computer, an analog quantity needs to be converted into digital values first. This conversion is achieved through a process known as sampling, which involves measuring and recording sound values at regular intervals. If the interval T between measurements is extremely short, the recorded discrete values will be very close to the analog signal, as shown in Fig. 1.6. After being converted to digital values, sound can be processed by using various calculations in a computer.

An image such as a photograph is converted into a collection of "points" called "pixels" first and then the color of each pixel is converted to a numeric value. For a monochrome image (i.e. a single color image, often in black and white), the color of one pixel is represented by one number. For example, 0 represents pure black, 255 represents pure white, and the degree of black between pure black and pure white is divided into 254 levels and represented by one number between 1 and 254.

For a color image, the color of one pixel is represented by a set of three numbers. In the RGB system (Fig. 1.7), the three numbers represent the respective ratios of the three primary colors of light: red (R), green (G), and blue (B). Figure 1.8 illustrates how the color purple is represented in the RGB system. In systems other than RGB, one number may represent brightness and the other two numbers may represent the color. Motion pictures, or videos, are decomposed into multiple images first and then processed in the same way as processing images.

Fig. 1.7 Three primary colors of light (RGB)

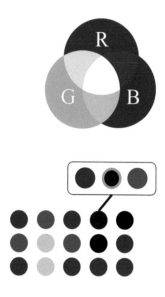

Fig. 1.8 Representing the color purple in the RGB system

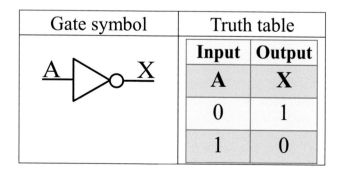

1.7 Computing Mechanism of a Computer

The interior of a computer comprises a multitude of arithmetic circuits. In these circuits, there are many electronic logic gates performing specific operations of "0" and "1" [2].

A combinational logic circuit is a kind of circuit whose output is determined by only the current input. The three most basic logic gates in combinational circuits are NOT, AND, and OR. Their definitions are given in Figs. 1.9, 1.10 and 1.11. In the figures, a truth table means a table showing the corresponding input–output values.

A logic gate performs logic operation, which involves only binary values 0 and 1. Logic NOT has only one input. It outputs the inverse value of the input. If the input is 0, the output will be 1. If the input is 1, the output will be 0.

Gate symbol	Truth table	
	Input	**Output**
A ▷o X	**A**	**X**
	0	1
	1	0

Fig. 1.9 Gate symbol and truth table of logic NOT

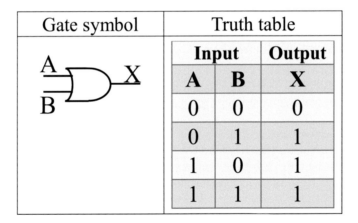

Gate symbol	Truth table		
	Input		**Output**
	A	**B**	**X**
	0	0	0
	0	1	0
	1	0	0
	1	1	1

Fig. 1.10 Gate symbol and truth table of logic AND

Gate symbol	Truth table		
	Input		**Output**
	A	**B**	**X**
	0	0	0
	0	1	1
	1	0	1
	1	1	1

Fig. 1.11 Gate symbol and truth table of logic OR

Logic AND has two inputs. If either of them is 0, the output will be 0. Only when both inputs are 1 will the output be 1. In other words, 0 AND 0 = 0, 0 AND 1 = 0, 1 AND 0 = 0, and 1 AND 1 = 1. These equations are the expressions of the logic AND operation, similar to the expressions of mathematical multiplication: $0 \times 0 = 0$, $0 \times 1 = 0$, $1 \times 0 = 0$, and $1 \times 1 = 1$. It should be noted that while logic AND and mathematical multiplication share similarities, they are not identical because logic AND operates with only binary values.

Logic OR has two inputs. If either of them is 1, the output will be 1. Only when both inputs are 0 will the output be 0. In other words, 0 OR 0 = 0, 0 OR 1 = 1, 1 OR 0 = 1, and 1 OR 1 = 1. These equations are the expressions of the logic OR operation, similar to the expressions of mathematical addition: $0 + 0 = 0$, $0 + 1 = 1$, $1 + 0 = 1$, and $1 + 1 = 2$.

Circuit symbols	Truth table			
	Input		**Output**	
	A	**B**	**C**	**S**
	0	0	0	0
	0	1	0	1
	1	0	0	1
	1	1	1	0

Fig. 1.12 Circuit symbols and the truth table of a half adder

While some logic operations yield the same result as mathematical calculations, it is essential to note that logic operations exclusively deal with binary values and serve fundamentally different purposes from mathematical calculations. Logic operations and mathematical calculations can be considered as two different computing systems.

By combining basic logic gates, a wide array of calculations can be performed. For example, the addition of two bits A and B can be realized by the circuit shown in Fig. 1.12. The sum of A and B is represented by S (Sum). Since S is only one bit, the sum "2" resulting from the addition "1 + 1" cannot be represented because every bit in a computer can only hold a value of either 0 or 1. Therefore, the digit increase C (Carry) is needed. The truth table for inputs A and B and outputs C and S is shown in Fig. 1.12. This circuit is called a "half adder" and is used for the first digit of addition. A full adder, which includes a carry input from the lower digit, can be realized by using two half adders.

In some circuits, past output is used as input to determine the current output. If the output of a circuit depends on its past output, the circuit is called a flip-flop. A flip-flop circuit has the ability to store information. For example, in the RS flip-flop circuit shown in Fig. 1.13, the current output Q is the result of applying OR then NOT to the current input R and the past output $\overline{Q}$, and the current output $\overline{Q}$ is the result of applying OR then NOT to the current input S and the past output Q. Such a circuit that depends on the past output is called a sequential circuit.

Complex processing is achieved by combining a large number of combinational logic circuits and sequential circuits. The integrated circuits introduced in Sect. 1.4 are combinations of many such circuits.

Exercises

1. Create the truth table for multiplying two bits.

Fig. 1.13 An RS flip-flop
circuit

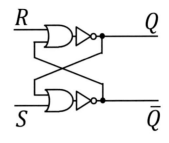

• **Guidance**
You may refer to the truth table for adding two bits (Fig. 1.12). In Fig. 1.12,
when A is 0 and B is 0, S is 0 because 0 (A) + 0 (B) = 0 (S). When A is 0 and
B is 1, S is 1 because 0 (A) + 1 (B) = 1 (S). When A is 1 and B is 0, S is 1
because 1 (A) + 0 (B) = 1 (S). When A is 1 and B is 1, the result is 2 because
1 (A) + 1 (B) = 2 (S). However, S cannot be 2 because there are only 0 and
1 in a computer. In this case, carry C is needed. Hence, in a computer, "10"
represents 2.

Similarly, when creating the truth table for multiplying two bits, first create
the input, for example, A and B. Then create the output and name it using an
alphabet. Since both A and B can be either 0 or 1, the table should have $2^2 =$
4 rows, as shown in Table 1.1. Fill in the values of each cell in the table. If one
column of output is enough, there is no need to create two columns.

Table 1.1 Truth table to complete for exercise problem 1

Input		Output
A	**B**	

2. Create the truth table for the circuit shown in Fig. 1.14.

Fig. 1.14 Circuit for
exercise problem 2

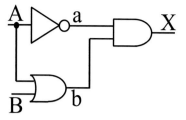

Table 1.2 Truth table to complete for exercise problem 2

Input		Output
A	**B**	**X**

• Guidance

The following is an example of how to get X:

   i. Let "a" be the result of NOT A, as shown in Fig. 1.14

  ii. Let "b" be the result of A OR B, as shown in Fig. 1.14

 iii. Then X is the result of "a" AND "b"

 iv. Both A and B can be either 0 or 1, so the table should have $2^2 = 4$ rows. Calculate X for each of the four input patterns.

Table 1.2 shows the table you should create. Please fill in the values into empty cells. If you find it difficult to get X directly from A and B, you may add two columns, "a" and "b", as shown in Table 1.3. For each input pattern, you can calculate "a" and "b" first, and then you can get X. For example, when A is 0 and B is 0, a = Not A (Not 0) = 1. b = A OR B (0 OR 0) = 0. As a result, X = a AND b (1 AND 0) = 0. Fill in the next three rows by yourself.

*3. Create the truth table for A AND B AND C.

*4. Create the truth table for NOT (A AND (B OR C)).

*5. Create a circuit for NOT (A AND (B OR C)) by using the gate symbols shown in Figs. 1.9, 1.10 and 1.11.

Problems marked with an asterisk "*" are optional. However, learners are encouraged to work on them independently to enhance their understanding and skills.

Table 1.3 Truth table to help solve exercise problem 2

Input				Output
A	**B**	**a**	**b**	**X**
0	0	1	0	0

References

1. Brookshear G, Brylow D (2014) Computer science: an overview, 12th edn. Pearson, Reading, MA
2. Petzold C (2000) Code: the hidden language of computer hardware and software. Microsoft Press, Redmond, WA

Chapter 2
Flowchart

2.1 What is a Flowchart

A program may be understandable by only developers and engineers. In contrast, a flowchart is a diagrammatic method that enables anyone to understand a program or calculation procedure. In this book, we will use flowcharts to explain many calculation procedures.

In a flowchart, each step is expressed by a box and the flow is shown by arrows between boxes. For example, Fig. 2.1 is a flowchart of the Java program shown in Fig. 1.3. In the flowchart, "Integer $a = 5$" corresponds to "int $a = 5$" in the program, "Integer $b = 3$" corresponds to "int $b = 3$" in the program, and "Output the sum of a and b" corresponds to "System.out. println($a + b$)" in the program. Since the steps in the flowchart are easily understandable, anyone reading it can grasp the program's functionality.

Initially used in the field of programming, flowchart is now widely used in various fields. For example, Fig. 2.2 is a flowchart illustrating the procedure of washing hands. First, wet your hands with water. Next, lather them with soap. Then, rinse off the soap with water. Afterward, check if your hands are clean. If yes, dry your hands with a towel and stop. Otherwise, repeat the above process.

A flowchart containing business details is useful in discussions with business partners and can often be understood more easily than a spoken explanation. It is important that the statements in a flowchart should be both concise and clear in meaning, as shown in Fig. 2.2.

Typical "boxes" in a flowchart include terminals, input/output, decision, and processes [1]. Figure 2.3 shows the symbols of these boxes. It should be noted that the symbols are predetermined and constant. "Start" and "end" are called terminals and should be oval. It is highly recommended to use them, because they serve as clear entry and exit points for the flowchart. Input and output are optional and should be parallelograms. Input refers to information going into the computer, such as data from the user. Output shows the result of a calculation or a message on the

© The Author(s), under exclusive license to Springer Nature Singapore Pte Ltd. 2024
W. Weng, *A Beginner's Guide to Informatics and Artificial Intelligence*,
https://doi.org/10.1007/978-981-97-1477-3_2

Fig. 2.1 A flowchart for the
program shown in Fig. 1.3

Fig. 2.2 A flowchart of
washing hands

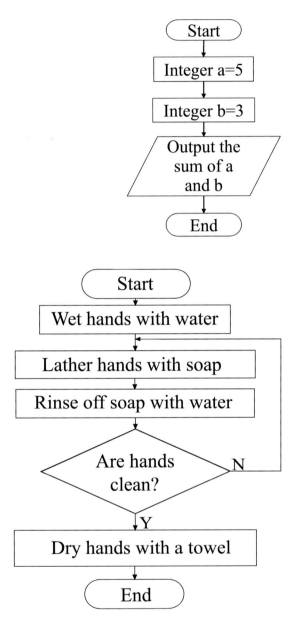

display. Decision is optional but is often used. A decision box should be a diamond and should have two output arrows, which typically represent the answers "yes" and "no". Process boxes are required. A process box should be a rectangular in which details of a step are described.

Fig. 2.3 Typical boxes in a
flowchart

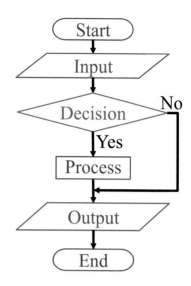

2.2 How to Create a Flowchart

The general approach to create a flowchart is explained using Fig. 2.4, a flowchart
of calculating the sum of integers 1 to n.

First, determine whether input and output are necessary. To get the sum of n
integers, n should be specified by the user, so input is necessary. The sum should
be displayed, so output is also necessary. As a result, create the boxes "input n" and
"output s (sum)". Then initialize variables, i.e. set the initial value of every variable
used in a flowchart. The output "s" is a variable (the reason why s is a variable will
be given later) and hence should be initialized. "$s = 0$" is its initialization, which
sets the initial value of s to 0. After initialization, create process boxes to detail the
calculation procedure.

To calculate "$1 + 2 + 3 + \ldots$", a variable i should be created to represent each
integer such as 1, 2, and 3. "$i = 1$" sets the initial value of i to 1. After initializing i,
the calculation procedure starts.

The meaning of the symbol "=" in a flowchart is to assign the value on the right
side to the variable on the left side. If the right side is a number, the number is
assigned directly to the variable on the left side, as exemplified in the steps "$s = 0$"
and "$i = 1$". If the right side is a formula, then calculate the formula first and then
assign the result to the variable on the left side, as exemplified in the step "$s = s +
i$". This step calculates "$s + i$" first and then assigns the result to s. Since the initial
value of s is 0 and the initial value of i is 1, this step calculates "$0 + 1$" first and then
assigns the result 1 to s. In other words, after executing this step, s changes from 0
to 1. Therefore, s is a variable that stores the sum of integers 1 to i.

If $n > 1$, the next step will be adding 2 to s. Since the current value of i is 1, it
should be increased by 1 so that i can represent 2. This is achieved by the step "i

Fig. 2.4 A flowchart of calculating the sum of integers 1 to *n*

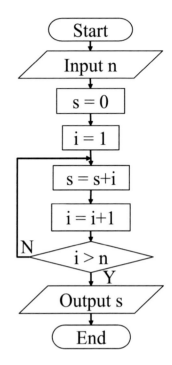

= *i* + 1". Then create a decision box to check if the current value of *i* has reached *n*. Supposing that *n* is 10, then the current value of *i*, 2, has not reached *n*, so the procedure exits the decision box from the arrow "no" and returns to "*s* = *s* + *i*". As a result, "*s* = *s* + *i*" will be executed again. This time, the step adds 2 to *s* and updates *s* with the result 3. Hence, after executing this step, *s* becomes the sum of integers 1 to 2.

The process of increasing *i* by 1 and adding it to *s* will be repeated until *i* becomes greater than *n*. When *i* becomes *n* + 1, the procedure will exit the decision box from "yes" and output *s*.

Statements in a flowchart can be conveyed through textual descriptions as shown in Fig. 2.2, or through the use of variables as illustrated in Fig. 2.4. When conveying numerical information, variables are commonly employed due to their ability to provide concise and precise representation compared to words. A flowchart can incorporate a blend of textual descriptions and variables, as exemplified in Fig. 2.5, a flowchart of taking fitness training ten times.

2.3   Notes on Flowcharting

Flowcharts created by beginners often have problems. Here are some notes you should pay attention to when creating flowcharts.

Fig. 2.5 A flowchart of
taking fitness training 10
times

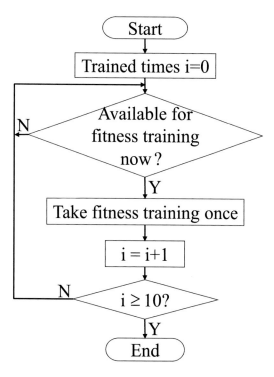

First, a decision box typically presents a yes/no question and has two output arrows corresponding to the answers to that question. Hence, create a question that can be answered by yes or no for each decision box. If a decision cannot be made with a simple yes/no answer, consider using multiple yes/no questions, as exemplified in Fig. 2.6. A decision box should have one more output arrow than the other boxes, so make sure to include the second output arrow. It is easy for beginners to believe that the box has been completed after drawing only one output arrow. In addition, make sure to label the two arrows "yes" and "no". If you revise the question in a decision box or the steps connected to it, check again if the labels "yes" and "no" are still correct after the update. It often happens that the labels become reversed after updating some boxes.

Second, do not write more than one question in a decision box. If you have multiple questions, create multiple decision boxes and write one question in each of them. For example, if you want to express three cases: $i < 10$, $i = 10$, and $i > 10$, avoid creating a flowchart like the one depicted in Fig. 2.6a; instead, create it in the way shown in Fig. 2.6b.

Third, boxes other than decision boxes should typically have a single output from the bottom. Having two or more outputs can lead to confusion, as it implies simultaneous execution of multiple steps, which contrasts with the purpose of a flowchart—to illustrate the sequential order of execution.

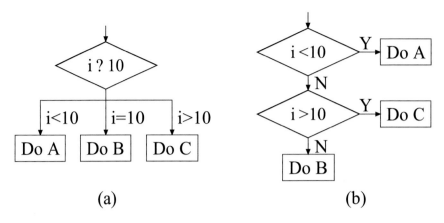

(a)   (b)

Fig. 2.6 An example of using multiple decision boxes

Last, it is generally preferred that arrows enter boxes from the top, rather than from the left or right side. This creates a visual hierarchy that aligns with the top-to-bottom reading habit in many cultures, improving clarity and understanding. Figure 2.7 shows two examples in which arrows enter boxes from the top and the right side, respectively. While it is true that many drawing software programs allow arrows to enter boxes from the left or right side, this flexibility is often provided to accommodate various diagramming needs. It is important to ensure that the flowchart remains clear and understandable.

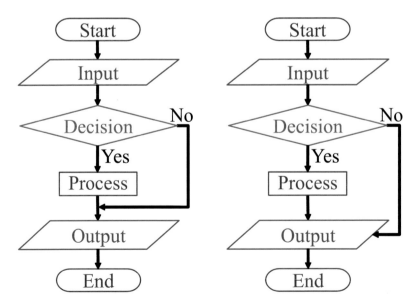

Fig. 2.7 Examples of arrows entering boxes

2.4 Clarify the Meaning of Each Statement

A flowchart should be easily understandable and free from ambiguity. Each statement should have a clear and singular meaning.

For example, using a single word like "jump" in a process box can lead to confusion. Is it a forward jump or upward? With one foot or two? For how long or how many times? In contrast, a statement such as "jump up once with both feet" will clear up most of the confusion. As another example, using "cook" as a process box is insufficient because it lacks specificity. It would be much clearer to provide details such as "bake at 230° for 10 s".

Similarly, ensure clarity in decision criteria. Avoid creating conditions that are hard to judge. For example, a question like "Is it late?" is insufficient because the criteria for "late" are unclear. In contrast, a condition such as "Is it later than 9 p.m.?" would be much better.

In short, a good flowchart should enable the reader to understand and execute its instructions with clarity and ease.

Exercises

1. Create a flowchart detailing a jumping exercise procedure where you should jump up either 15 times or for 20 s, whichever comes first.

> **• Guidance**
>
> Some learners may create a flowchart like the one shown in Fig. 2.8. The figure lacks details, but if you create a similar flowchart, there is room for improvement. Figure 2.8 has many problems, such as having two output arrows exiting a box that is not a decision box. We discussed this problem in Sect. 2.3. Non-decision boxes should have only one output because multiple outputs cannot be executed simultaneously. Therefore, it is better to use a single output and evaluate the two conditions sequentially.
>
> In addition, the steps required before you can tell the answers to the two questions are not included in Fig. 2.8. If you do not count, you will not know if 15 times have been reached. The procedure of counting should be included in the flowchart. You may refer to the way of writing in Fig. 2.5. You may use i as the counter and after each jump, increase i by 1. By comparing i with 15, you can know if 15 times have been reached. Since i is a variable, you should initialize it first. Similarly, you should create a step for setting a timer or an alarm so that you can know if 20 s are reached. If you write all these details, you will get the full score.

The exercises in this and subsequent chapters serve the dual purpose of assessing your understanding and enhancing problem-solving abilities. It is crucial to develop the skills to apply classroom knowledge to unfamiliar problems. Although it

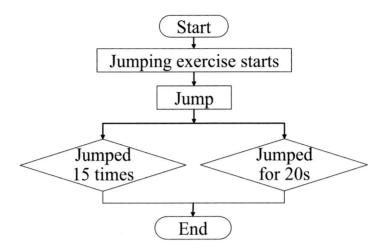

Fig. 2.8 A flowchart created by some learners

may be challenging initially, dedicated effort often leads to greater-than-expected achievements.

Reference

1. Andersen B, Fagerhaug T, Henriksen B, Onsøyen LE (2008) Mapping work processes, 2nd edn. ASQ Quality Press, Milwaukee

Chapter 3
Time Complexity

3.1 What is Time Complexity

Computers execute calculations based on programs, making programs the key determinant of computational efficiency. One way to evaluate program efficiency is by considering its time complexity.

Time complexity is expressed using the big O notation [1]. $O(n)$ is read "big O of n", where O is called order and n is called size. In many cases, size is determined by the amount of input data, so $O(n)$ represents the time needed to process n data. In the big O notation, "$O()$" is a constant factor whereas "n" is a variable that varies depending on the specific problem. The method to get n is: (1) use a polynomial of n to express the number of instructions to be executed, (2) find in the polynomial the term that has the biggest effect, and (3) change the term's coefficient to 1. The resultant monomial is what should be placed within the "()" after the big O. In the following, we give detailed examples of getting the polynomial of instructions using a flowchart.

3.2 How to Know Time Complexity from a Flowchart

Time complexity can be obtained from the flowchart of a program or calculation procedure. We use the flowchart of calculating the sum of integers 1 to n as an example to explain this.

When the calculation procedure depicted in Fig. 3.1 is executed, part (4), comprising 3 instructions, is triggered each time an integer is added to s. Since a total of n integers are added, part (4) is executed n times. As a result, the number of instructions to be executed in part (4) is $3 \times n = 3n$. The remaining 4 instructions are (1), (2), (3), and (5). The terminals "start" and "end" are not typically counted as instructions. Instead, they serve as entry and exit points like boundary markers for

Fig. 3.1 Flowchart of
getting the sum of integers 1
to n

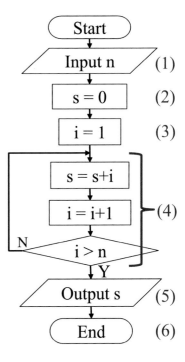

the flowchart. Combined with part (4), the total number of instructions is $3n + 4$.
Therefore, $3n + 4$ is the polynomial representing the number of instructions.

For the $3n + 4$ instructions, if the execution time of each instruction is U, the total
execution time will be $(3n + 4) \times U$. When n is sufficiently large, the constant 4
will be negligible and the term $3n$ will have the biggest effect on the execution time.
Replace the coefficient of $3n$ with 1 and place the result n within the parentheses of
$O()$. As a result, the time complexity of the flowchart is $O(n)$.

Figure 3.2 is an example of a flowchart with a time complexity of $O(n^2)$. To
determine the number of instructions in the flowchart, start by examining the central
blue solid-line loop, as it undergoes the most iterations. The loop, comprising 3
instructions (steps ① to ③), is executed n times, starting with j initialized to n (step
2) and concluding when j reaches 1 (step ③). Accordingly, the total number of
instructions in the loop is $3 \times n = 3n$.

Then look at the pink dashed-line loop. The number of instructions in this loop
is $3n + 4$, including the instructions in the blue solid-line loop, $3n$, and 4 other
instructions (steps 1–4). This loop undergoes n iterations, starting with i initialized
to n (step II) and concluding when i reaches 1 (step 4). Accordingly, the total number
of instructions in this loop is $(3n + 4) \times n = 3n^2 + 4n$. The number of instructions
outside this loop is 3 (steps I–III). As a result, the total number of instructions is $3n^2$
$+ 4n + 3$. This is the polynomial representing the number of instructions.

When n is sufficiently large, the term with the biggest impact on execution time
is $3n^2$, rendering $4n$ and 3 negligible. Replace the coefficient of $3n^2$ with 1 and place

Fig. 3.2 A flowchart whose
time complexity is $O(n^2)$

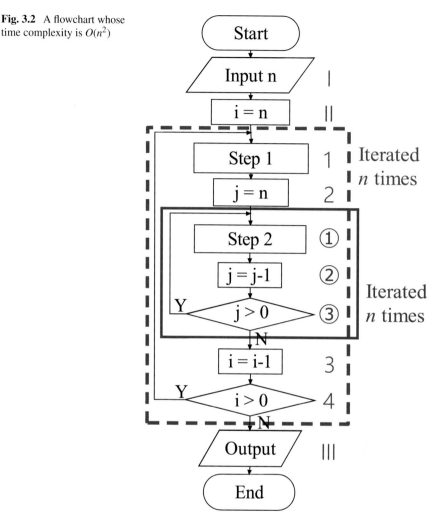

the result n^2 within the parentheses after the big O. Hence, the time complexity of
this flowchart is $O(n^2)$.

Based on the above two examples, the relation between a flowchart and the number
of instructions can be described as follows: if a flowchart contains an i-fold loop,
in which C instructions are iterated n times, then there will be a term $C \times n^i$ in
the polynomial representing the total number of instructions. The instructions not
contained in any loops will contribute a constant term to the polynomial. As a result,
when trying to get the time complexity from a flowchart, find the loop that is iterated
the most. If the number of iterations R of the loop is n^i, the time complexity will be
$O(n^i)$.

What will happen if the number of iterations R of a loop is not exactly n^i? Consider the flowchart in Fig. 3.3, which contains a single loop. The loop is iterated $n^2 - 1$ times and contains C_1 instructions. Immediately preceding the loop, C_0 instructions are executed, and immediately after the loop, C_2 instructions are executed. In total, there are $(n^2 - 1)C_1 + C_0 + C_2 + 2$ instructions. As a result, the polynomial representing the number of instructions is

$$E = (n^2 - 1)C_1 + C_0 + C_2 + 2$$
$$= C_1 n^2 - C_1 + C_0 + C_2 + 2.$$

Accordingly, the time complexity is $O(n^2)$. In conclusion, whether the number of iterations R of the most iterated loop is exactly n^i or a polynomial where n^i is the biggest item, the time complexity will be $O(n^i)$. If the number of iterations R of the loop is a constant, the number of instructions will be a constant. In such a case, the time complexity is expressed by $O(1)$, which means constant time.

Fig. 3.3 A flowchart where a loop is iterated R times

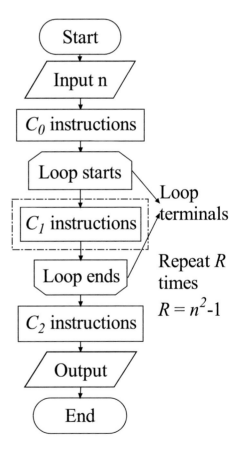

3.3 Significance of Time Complexity

Time complexity represents how the time required to solve a problem will increase as the problem size increases. The big O notation is a concise notation that describes the upper bound of complexity in relation to input data size n [2].

The following is a comparison of efficiency between two programs whose time complexities are $O(n)$ and $O(n^2)$, respectively. Consider the polynomials representing the number of instructions as $E_1(n) = C_{1,1}n + C_{1,2}$ and $E_2(n) = C_{2,1}n^2 + C_{2,2}n + C_{2,3}$. Even if $C_{1,1}$ and $C_{1,2}$ are much greater than $C_{2,1}$, $C_{2,2}$, and $C_{2,3}$, for sufficiently large n, $E_1(n)$ will always be smaller than $E_2(n)$. For example, with $E_1(n) = 999n + 1000$ and $E_2(n) = n^2$, whenever $n > 1000$, $E_1(n)$ is consistently smaller than $E_2(n)$, as illustrated in Fig. 3.4.

This indicates that a program's execution time depends on the exponential term rather than the coefficient or constant in the polynomial representing the number of instructions. In addition, error in execution time may affect the coefficients and constants but not the exponential term. As a result, a program with a time complexity of $O(n)$ is more efficient than one with a time complexity of $O(n^2)$. In other words, the less the time complexity is, the higher the efficiency will be [3]. If two programs are the same in time complexity, comparison of efficiency should be made based on the number of instructions, coefficients, and constants.

Time complexity is an important measure. As computers advance in speed and capability, time complexity governs the execution speed as problem size grows. When

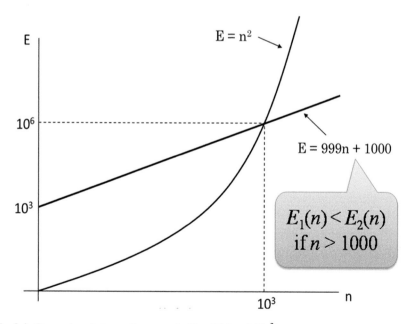

Fig. 3.4 Comparison between time complexities $O(n)$ and $O(n^2)$

dealing with small problem sizes, it might not be so important to discuss efficiency. This is because even the most inefficient program can be executed almost instantly, making execution time a non-issue. However, as problem sizes increase, it becomes crucial to consider how execution time scales and whether it remains within practical limits.

3.4 How to Evaluate a Program

How to evaluate if a program is good or not? The following is a list of evaluation criteria.

(1) Less Execution Time

A good program should be executable within a short time. The execution time is largely determined by time complexity. For example, if one program outputs the result immediately, whereas another program does not output the result after 20 min, the former is clearly better.

(2) Less Memory (Storage Space) Required

A program that requires less memory (storage space) is superior to one that requires more. For example, a program that can be executed with 1 GB (gigabytes) of memory is better than one requiring 5 GB, because a computer with 4 GB memory can run only the former.

(3) Easy to Understand

A program that is easy to understand is better than one that is not. Creating a program does not necessarily mean it is complete. Bugs are often discovered and fixed later, and changes may be necessary due to evolving circumstances. Therefore, a good program should have a well-structured design with sufficient comments, making it easy to understand and maintain.

Various criteria are considered when assessing the quality of a program. Criterion (3), easy to understand, holds significant importance, but it often depends on individual perspectives and is challenging to quantify. The emphasis on criterion (2), less memory required, has diminished over time due to advancements in semiconductor technology, which have made memory both cheaper and larger in capacity. As a result, criterion (1), execution time, or time complexity, currently takes precedence as the primary criterion for program evaluation, as it allows for quantitative assessment.

Exercises

1. What is the time complexity if the polynomial representing the number of instructions is $8n^3 + 10000n + 83{,}417$?

Fig. 3.5 Flowchart for
exercise problem 3

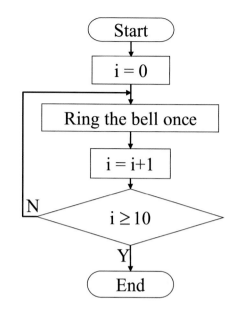

2. What is the time complexity if the number of instructions E satisfies $2n^2 - 100 \geq E \geq 100n + 12{,}345$?

• **Guidance**
You can plot the lower bound and upper bound formulas on the X and Y axes. You will find the result similar to Fig. 3.4. In the figure, focus on the range when n is very large and find the polynomial that represents the largest possible case of n, as time complexity is used to reflect the time required when n is at its maximum. Consider the term with the biggest effect in that polynomial.

---

3. Find the time complexity of the flowchart shown in Fig. 3.5.

• **Guidance**
You may refer to the paragraph right before Sect. 3.3, a summary of the relation between the number of iterations and time complexity.

---

*4. What is the time complexity if the number of instructions E satisfies $(3\log n)n + 100 \geq E \geq 5\log n - 19$?

*5. Find the time complexity of the flowchart in Fig. 3.6.

Fig. 3.6 Flowchart for
exercise problem 5

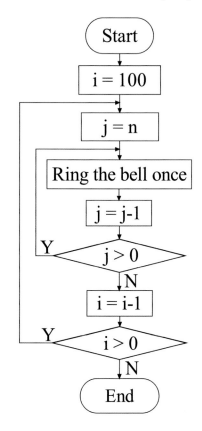

References

1. Levitin A (2011) Introduction to the design and analysis of algorithms. Addison Wesley Publishing Company, London
2. Huang S (2020) What is big O notation: space and time complexity. https://www.freecodecamp.org/news/big-o-notation-why-it-matters-and-why-it-doesnt-1674cfa8a23c/
3. Zindros D (2012) A gentle introduction to algorithm complexity analysis. https://discrete.gr/complexity/

Chapter 4
Artificial Intelligence—Mathematical Modeling

4.1 What is Artificial Intelligence

The significance of mathematical modeling lies in its necessity before applying artificial intelligence (AI) to solve optimization problems.

AI is a popular field that attempts to use computers to achieve human-like intelligence. AI techniques can be broadly divided into two categories: knowledge-based techniques such as expert systems and soft computing techniques such as genetic algorithms and machine learning. In expert systems, knowledge bases serve as databases housing rules that emulate the decision-making processes employed by human experts. The rules are often expressed in the form "if A, then B", where A is the phenomenon and B is the conclusion, solution, or recommendation. Reasoning engines derive answers from the user input and knowledge bases. If the user input is A, then B will be displayed if it corresponds to A in the knowledge bases. Expert systems have been widely used for diagnosing machine failures and biological diseases. After inputting the symptom, the system will show the cause of a failure or the name of a disease.

Soft computing techniques use computers to study, model, analyze, and estimate complex events. There are many soft computing techniques such as genetic algorithms, machine learning, and fuzzy logic. In this textbook, we will introduce genetic algorithms and neural networks, two popular and widely applicable techniques for solving various problems. Genetic algorithm is one of the most typical evolutionary and heuristic search methods, which are used for optimization problems. Neural network, on the other hand, is typical for machine learning and deep learning, which are used for pattern recognition, classification, natural language processing, computer vision, etc. They represent two different AI domains and have numerous real-world applications. They can serve as stepping stones for learners to delve deeper into AI and related fields. That being said, AI is a rapidly evolving field and there are many other AI approaches worth exploring as well.

© The Author(s), under exclusive license to Springer Nature Singapore Pte Ltd. 2024
W. Weng, *A Beginner's Guide to Informatics and Artificial Intelligence*,
https://doi.org/10.1007/978-981-97-1477-3_4

4.2 Target Problems of AI Optimization Methods

AI optimization methods such as genetic algorithms are widely used to solve NP-hard (Non-deterministic Polynomial-time hard) optimization problems. An optimization problem aims to find the best solution, namely the optimal solution, among many candidate solutions.

One of the methods is called exhaustive search, which checks all the candidate solutions to identify the optimal one. As the problem size increases, it will become unrealistic for exhaustive search to find in a reasonable time the optimal solution. In such a case, the problem is often called NP-hard. Though time complexity is not the sole criterion, it is often observed that if the time complexity of solving a problem using exhaustive search is $O(n^2)$ or greater, such as $O(n^3)$ or $O(n!)$, the problem is typically regarded as NP-hard.

There are many NP-hard optimization problems such as production scheduling problems, transportation routing problems, and asset allocating problems. Detailed examples are given in the following.

4.3 Mathematical Modeling of a Problem

To solve NP-hard optimization problems using AI, both mathematical modeling and encoding are necessary. This reliance stems from the fact that AI methods depend on computer-based computation. As previously introduced in Chap. 1, computers process all information using numerical data, necessitating the representation of problems in a numerical format. Creating the numerical format of a problem is referred to as "mathematical modeling" or simply "modeling" of the problem.

After completing the modeling of a problem, the process of expressing a candidate solution using a set of numerical values is referred to as "encoding". In the following, we will provide detailed explanations of how to perform mathematical modeling and encoding for two NP-hard optimization problems, respectively.

4.3.1 Single Machine Scheduling Problem

A set of jobs sharing a common due date will be processed on a single machine. Find the sequence for processing the jobs so that the total deviation between each job's completion time and the due date is minimized [1, 2].

Figure 4.1 illustrates this problem. The time axis is depicted horizontally. It shows the sequence of processing the jobs, along with each job's start time, processing time, and completion time. For example, the left endpoint of job 1 corresponds to its start time, and the right endpoint corresponds to its completion time. The span between these two points represents job 1's duration, i.e. processing time. The processing time

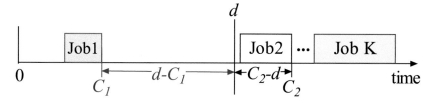

Fig. 4.1 Single machine scheduling problem

of each job and the due date are given in advance. Since the jobs are processed on a single machine, they cannot be processed simultaneously. Hence, at most one job can be completed exactly on the due date, which is considered the optimal scenario with a deviation of zero between the job's completion time and due date. The other jobs must be completed either earlier or later than the due date. If a job is completed earlier than the due date, such as job 1, the deviation is calculated as "due date-completion time". If a job is completed later than the due date, such as job 2, the deviation is calculated as "completion time-due date". In all the cases, the deviation will be no less than zero. The objective is to minimize the sum of these deviations for all the jobs.

Solving this problem has important real-world implications. In a factory, a job represents an unfinished product that may start as raw material and finish as a product. Regardless of whether a job is completed before or after its due date, costs are incurred. If a job is completed earlier than the due date, it will become inventory and lead to inventory costs, which encompass expenses related to storage space and management. If a job is completed later than the due date, it will incur delay costs, including fines, potential loss of future orders due to customer dissatisfaction, and idling costs in the subsequent production processes if the completed jobs (semi-products) are delivered there late. Accordingly, completing all the jobs as close as possible to their due dates will minimize the combined inventory and delay costs, and hence is known as the optimal solution.

The single machine scheduling problem is a simplified mathematical model that mirrors such real-world problems. In the single machine scheduling problem, all jobs share a common due date for completion. Completing a job ahead of the due date incurs inventory costs, while finishing it late results in delay costs. Minimizing the total deviation between each job's completion time and the due date will minimize the total inventory and delay costs. Since the deviation between a job's completion time and the due date is determined by the sequence in which the jobs are processed, the objective is to find the optimal processing sequence—a sequence where the total deviation is at its minimum. This optimal sequence is referred to as the optimal solution to the problem.

Mathematical modeling involves three key elements: notation, objective function, and constraints. Notation refers to creating names and assigning numerical values to them to represent essential information for solving a problem. Objective function is typically a formula used to evaluate the quality of a solution, aiming to either maximize or minimize a specific metric. Constraints are the conditions a solution must meet when applicable. The outcome is known as the mathematical model of the problem.

The following is an example of the mathematical model of the single machine scheduling problem.

Notation

d common due date
i index of job ($i = 1, 2, ..., K$)
C_i completion time of job i
P_i processing time of job i

$$\text{Objective function: Minimize } \sum_{i=1}^{K} |C_i - d| \qquad (4.1)$$

In the notation, d represents the common due date, i.e. the time that all the jobs are desired to be completed. i represents index of job, ranging from 1 to K for K jobs. C_i represents the completion time of job i, and P_i represents the processing time of job i.

In the objective function, $C_i - d$ represents the deviation between a job's completion time and the due date when the job is completed after the due date. If a job is completed before the due date, the deviation will be $d - C_i$. Therefore, $|C_i - d|$ represents the deviation between a job's completion time and the due date, regardless of whether the job is completed before or after the due date. We sum up these deviations using sigma "$\sum$", and the objective is to minimize this total deviation.

• Questions

1. If there are n jobs and the first job starts processing at time 0, with each subsequent job starting immediately after the previous job is completed, how many possible processing sequences are there?

   Hint: if there are n jobs, how many jobs among them can be processed first? After processing the first job, how many jobs can be processed the second? How many jobs can be processed the third? This pattern continues until the job that can be processed the nth. In total, what is the number of processing sequences?

2. What is the time complexity of solving this problem using exhaustive search? (Exhaustive search calculates the objective function values for all processing sequences to find the one with the smallest value.)

Hint: you may consider the number of iterations of the objective function value calculation loop within the exhaustive search flowchart (Fig. 4.2). As discussed in Chap. 3, you can know the time complexity from the number of iterations of the loop.

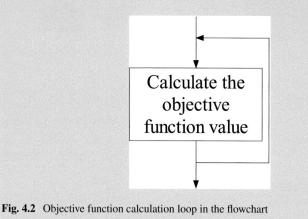

Fig. 4.2 Objective function calculation loop in the flowchart

Based on the answers to questions 1 and 2, the single machine scheduling problem is considered NP-hard, and the reasons are as follows.

The "problem size" mentioned in Sect. 4.2 is determined by the number of jobs in this problem. If the number of jobs is n, the number of processing sequences, or candidate solutions, will be ( ), which is an exponentially growing value. A problem that aims to find the optimal solution among these candidates is called an optimization problem.

Exhaustive search examines all candidate solutions by calculating their objective function values to identify the optimal solution. While this method guarantees finding the optimal solution, it becomes impractical as the number of jobs increases. For example, with 100 jobs, the number of candidate solutions will be ( ), which is astronomical. Calculating the objective function value for each of them could take days or even weeks, which is not feasible in most real-world scenarios where jobs must start processing shortly after being received. Such a problem that requires an unrealistic amount of time for exhaustive search is typically an "NP-hard problem".

The following is another example of an NP-hard optimization problem.

4.3.2 Knapsack Problem

Given a knapsack and a set of items, each with a size and a value, find the items to be put into the knapsack so that the total value of the items in the knapsack is maximized.

Fig. 4.3 An example of items in the knapsack problem

A similar problem in our daily life could be that you are packing up before traveling (Fig. 4.3). You want to take many things, but the bag is limited in size, so you need to decide which items to choose.

The significance of solving the knapsack problem extends broadly, as it serves as a representative model for numerous real-life scenarios involving the optimization of value within constraints. For example, when using a certain area of land for agriculture, when using a certain area of land for construction, or when using a truck limited in size to transport goods, what should be chosen to maximize the profit? When using a certain amount of time to do part-time jobs, which part-time jobs will maximize the income? The strategies and techniques used to address the knapsack problem can be applied to solve these similar problems.

The following is an example of modeling the knapsack problem.

Notation

i index of item ($i = 1, 2, \ldots, K$)
S_i size of item i
S_n size of the knapsack
V_i value of item i
C_i $C_i = 1$, item i is in the knapsack
     $C_i = 0$, item i is not in the knapsack

$$\text{Objective function: Maximize} \sum_{i=1}^{K} V_i C_i \tag{4.2}$$

$$\text{Subject to:} \sum_{i=1}^{K} S_i C_i \leq S_n \tag{4.3}$$

In the notation, i represents index of item. If there are K items, the value of i will range from 1 to K. S_i represents size of item i, and S_n represents size of the knapsack. V_i represents value of item i. C_i is an integer being either 1 or 0. When it is 1, it means item i is included in the knapsack. When it is 0, it means item i is not included in the knapsack.

In the objective function, if item i is included in the knapsack, C_i is 1 and hence $V_i C_i$ is V_i. If item i is not included in the knapsack, C_i is 0 and hence $V_i C_i$ is 0. Therefore, $\sum_{i=1}^{K} V_i C_i$ represents the total value of the items in the knapsack, because the value of $V_i C_i$ for an item not in the knapsack is zero. The objective is to maximize this total value, so adding "maximize" before $\sum_{i=1}^{K} V_i C_i$ results in the objective function. Similar to what $\sum_{i=1}^{K} V_i C_i$ represents, $\sum_{i=1}^{K} S_i C_i$ represents the total size of the items included in the knapsack. This can be understood by replacing V_i with S_i in the above explanation. This size must not exceed the size capacity of the knapsack.

4.4 Encoding

To tackle such NP-hard optimization problems, AI optimization methods such as genetic algorithms are commonly employed. These methods prioritize finding high-quality solutions quickly, rather than seeking the optimal solution over an unreasonably long time. To apply AI optimization methods, in addition to mathematical modeling, encoding candidate solutions is necessary.

Encoding is a process of representing a candidate solution using a series of numerical values defined in the mathematical model. In Fig. 4.4, the series of numerical values on a pink background represents a candidate solution, referred to as an "individual" or a "chromosome" in genetic algorithms. Each bit in it, which is highlighted in yellow, is called a "gene" in genetic algorithms. The encoding task is to assign meanings to both the order and value of each bit in a candidate solution. For example, when the first bit has an order of 1 and a value of 3, you should define what these 1 and 3 mean respectively in the encoding process.

Figure 4.5 shows an example of encoding for the single machine scheduling problem. In this example, each bit's order represents the job's processing order, and its value represents the index of job. For example, the first bit with an order of 1 represents "processed the 1st", and the last bit with an order of K represents "processed the Kth". Similarly, the first bit's value of 3 represents job 3, and the last bit's value of 5 represents job 5. In other words, the first job to process is job 3, and the Kth job to process is job 5.

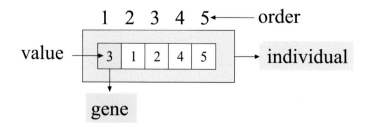

Fig. 4.4 An example of a candidate solution in genetic algorithms

Candidate   1 2 3 ... K ← order of processing
solution : | 3 | 1 | 2 | ... | 5 | ← index of job

Fig. 4.5 An example of encoding for the single machine scheduling problem

---

• Questions

3. What is the order of processing job 1 in the candidate solution shown in Fig. 4.5?
4. Which job is processed the third?

Methods of encoding for a given problem are not unique. For example, in Fig. 4.5, a bit's order can represent index of job, and its value can represent the order of processing. Different ways of encoding for the same problem may vary in computational efficiency.

Figure 4.6 is an example of encoding for the knapsack problem. A bit's order represents i—index of item, and its value represents C_i—whether the item is included in the knapsack. In this example, item 1 is not included in the knapsack, whereas item 2 is included.

• Questions

5. Is item 3 included in the knapsack in the candidate solution shown in Fig. 4.6?

Exercises

Salesman Problem

Given a set of cities and the distance between every two cities, find the shortest distance a salesman can visit all the cities one at a time.

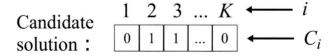

Candidate   1 2 3 ... K ←——— i
solution : | 0 | 1 | 1 | ... | 0 | ←——— C_i

Fig. 4.6 An example of encoding for the knapsack problem

• **Questions**

6. If there are *n* cities, how many possible routes exist to visit them all?

   Hint: the hints given for questions 1 and 2 before Sect. 4.3.2 are equally helpful for questions 6 and 7. Simply replace "jobs" with "cities" and "process" with "visit" in the hints.

7. What is the time complexity of solving this problem using exhaustive search?

Based on the answers to questions 6 and 7, the salesman problem is also considered an NP-hard problem, sharing similarities with the single machine scheduling problem. Therefore, instead of using exhaustive search, which can demand an impractical amount of computation time, AI optimization methods are often employed to swiftly obtain high-quality solutions. In the next chapter, we will detail how to apply genetic algorithms to solve this problem. As mentioned earlier, both mathematical modeling and encoding are prerequisites for applying AI optimization methods, so please proceed with the following tasks:

1. Mathematical modeling for this problem (create the notation and objective function)

• **Guidance**

Let us start with a brief explanation of the problem before delving into the exercise details. If we use one circle to represent one city, then the circles in Fig. 4.7 represent a set of cities. The distances between cities are given, corresponding to the lengths of the arcs between the circles.

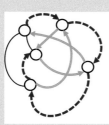

Notation

C city?

... ...

Objective function

Minimize $\sum_{i=1}^{4} distance$

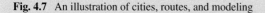

C1 C2

Fig. 4.7 An illustration of cities, routes, and modeling

The salesman can start from any city. For example, he can start from the upper-left city, move right, down, and up to reach the middle-left city, following the red dashed lines, which represent one possible route. Alternatively, he can start from the lower-left city, move up, down, right, and left to reach the upper-left city, following the blue lines, representing another possible route.

Between the above two routes, it seems that the one marked with red dashed lines is shorter, but there are many possible routes and the red dashed route may not be the shortest. The objective is to find the shortest route.

Now, let us delve into the exercise details. To model this problem, you need to establish the necessary notation and objective function. For example, you can use "C" to represent some city-related information. Please define all the notation and create the objective function, which should represent the total distance traveled by the salesman.

For example, consider the red dashed route, which can be broken down into the sum of four smaller distances. Each small distance can be expressed using the information associated with two cities, such as C1 and C2. In other words, begin by representing each small distance using the information of two cities, then sum the four small distances to calculate the entire distance. Finally, minimize the entire distance.

2. Encode candidate solutions for this problem (define what the order and value of each bit in a candidate solution represent).

• Guidance

You can proceed with encoding even if you have not completed the mathematical model. You may refer to the encoding example in Fig. 4.5, as it closely resembles an applicable way of encoding for this problem.

*3. Try providing a different way of encoding from the one you provided in exercise problem 2.

References

1. Tanaka S (2016) Single-machine scheduling problem with precedence constraints. https://sites.google.com/site/shunjitanaka/prec-single
2. Feldmann M, Biskup D (2003) Single-machine scheduling for minimizing earliness and tardiness penalties by meta-heuristic approaches. Comput Ind Eng 44(2):307–323

Chapter 5
Artificial Intelligence—Genetic Algorithm

5.1 What is Genetic Algorithm

Genetic algorithm (GA) is a biologically inspired search method used to find high-quality solutions for complex problems. As previously introduced in Chap. 4, exhaustive search is often impractical for solving NP-hard optimization problems, and GA is designed to quickly identify good solutions. GA can effectively tackle a large variety of NP-hard optimization problems, including the single machine scheduling problem, the knapsack problem, and the salesman problem discussed in Chap. 4.

5.2 Flowchart of Genetic Algorithm

Figure 5.1 depicts the basic flowchart of solving a problem using GA. The procedure begins by generating the initial population, which consists of individuals representing candidate solutions to the problem. Each individual is expressed by a set of numerical values, as explained in encoding (Sect. 4.4). In GA, the terms "individual", "candidate solution", and "chromosome" are used interchangeably. The initial population is also referred to as the first generation.

After creating the initial population, evaluate the fitness of each individual using the objective function established in the mathematical modeling introduced in Sect. 4. 3. For a maximization objective function, higher values indicate higher fitness, whereas for a minimization objective function, lower values indicate higher fitness.

Proceed by iteratively producing new generations using three operators: selection, crossover, and mutation [1]. When the termination criterion is met, output the objective function value of the best individual in the final generation as the result.

In the following, we give detailed explanations for each step by applying GA to solve the salesman problem introduced in the previous chapter.

© The Author(s), under exclusive license to Springer Nature Singapore Pte Ltd. 2024
W. Weng, *A Beginner's Guide to Informatics and Artificial Intelligence*,
https://doi.org/10.1007/978-981-97-1477-3_5

Fig. 5.1 Flowchart of
genetic algorithm

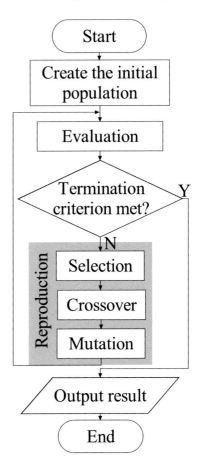

5.3   How to Use GA to Solve a Problem

Salesman problem

Given a set of cities and the distance between every two cities (Fig. 5.2), find the shortest distance a salesman can visit all the cities one at a time.

Let us start with a brief overview of this problem. In Fig. 5.2, each circle represents a city, and there are a total of four cities. The index of each city is the number inside the corresponding circle. The distances between cities are shown on the lines connecting them. For example, the distance between city 1 and city 2 is 18, and the distance between city 2 and city 4 is 6. We will use the mathematical model for this problem provided in the solutions to the previous chapter's exercises and the encoding shown in Fig. 5.3. In this encoding, the order of a bit represents i—order of visit, and the value of a bit represents C_i—ith city to visit.

Fig. 5.2 An example of the
salesman problem

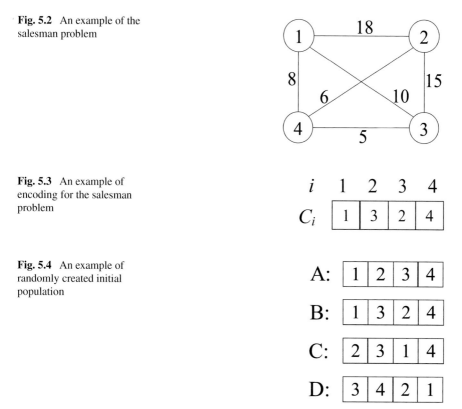

Fig. 5.3 An example of
encoding for the salesman
problem

Fig. 5.4 An example of
randomly created initial
population

5.3.1 Initial Population Creation

The initial population is often created randomly, usually consisting of 20 to 100
individuals, depending on the problem's size. Generally, the larger the problem size
is, the more individuals there would be in one generation.

In the salesman problem, the problem size is determined by the number of cities.
Since the number of cities in this example is 4, the total number of candidate solutions
is $4! = 24$ (explanation for this calculation can be found in the previous chapter). The
number of individuals in one generation is usually much less than the total number
of candidate solutions, so for this example, we choose to have 4 individuals in one
generation. Figure 5.4 shows the four randomly created individuals.

5.3.2 Evaluation

Evaluation is made by calculating the objective function value for each individual,
as shown in Fig. 5.5. For example, individual A represents the route that city 1 is

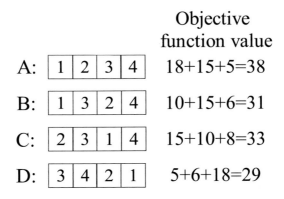

Fig. 5.5 Evaluation of the individuals

visited first, followed by city 2, city 3, and finally city 4. Since the distance between city 1 and city 2 is 18, between city 2 and city 3 is 15, and between city 3 and city 4 is 5, the total distance is $18 + 15 + 5 = 38$.

Since this is a minimization problem, individuals with smaller objective function values have higher fitness. Therefore, the fitness ranking of the four individuals is D > B > C > A.

5.3.3 Selection

Selection in GA mimics natural selection, favoring individuals with higher fitness for the next generation. Those selected individuals will continue to the next generation, whereas unselected ones will not. Multiple types of selections are often employed in one GA process. In the following, examples will be given to detail two common types of selections: elite selection and tournament selection.

5.3.3.1 Elite Selection

The word "elite" refers to the most outstanding individuals. Accordingly, elite selection selects individuals that are the highest in fitness. If i individuals are to be selected, then they will be the top i individuals. If multiple individuals share the same fitness as the ith individual, one will be selected randomly as the ith individual.

For example, we employ elite selection to select one individual from the initial population shown in Fig. 5.4. Individual D, the highest in fitness among the four individuals, will be selected. If multiple individuals have the same highest fitness, select one of them randomly. The selected individual D will be in the next generation.

The advantage of elite selection is that it ensures that the fittest individuals survive into the next generation, guaranteeing that the best individuals in the current generation are not lost in the evolutionary process. As a result, the best individual in the final generation will be the best individual in all the generations. Without elite selection, the best individual in the current generation may disappear in the next generation.

5.3.3.2 Tournament Selection

Tournament selection selects the winner from a tournament match between k individuals, where k is called tournament size, representing the number of participants in the match.

For example, we employ tournament selection with $k = 2$ to select one individual from the initial population shown in Fig. 5.4. We randomly pick up A and B as the two participants in the tournament. Among them, B has a higher fitness than A and hence will be selected. The selected individual B will become an individual in the next generation.

The advantage of tournament selection is that it offers flexibility in selecting individuals. As k increases, the probability of selecting highly fit individuals rises, whereas lower k values increase the chances of selecting less fit individuals. Adjusting k allows for the selection of individuals with varying fitness levels, contributing to diversity within a generation.

5.3.4 Crossover

Crossover is an operator that mimics the reproductive process in living organisms. Similar to human reproduction where two individuals, typically parents, produce offspring, crossover involves two individuals, with the child inheriting genes from its parents [2].

Crossover is assigned a crossover rate, analogous to a marriage or mating rate. Typically, the crossover rate is set relatively high, ranging from 75 to 95%. This ensures a sufficient number of offspring for a broader exploration of candidate solutions. If the crossover rate is too low, there will be less offspring, limiting the search for new individuals. However, a 100% crossover rate can lead to too rapid updates, potentially causing the loss of promising individuals before they can produce high-quality offspring.

While various types of selections are often employed, it is common to employ a single type of crossover in one GA process. The two most widely used types of crossovers are one-point crossover and two-point crossover.

For example, we perform one-point crossover with a crossover rate of 90% to produce one offspring from the initial population shown in Fig. 5.4. First, we randomly pick up two individuals as parents, in this case, C and D. Next, we generate

Fig. 5.6 An example of
one-point crossover

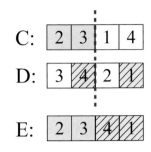

a random number r_1 to determine whether C and D will crossover. If you are implementing GA using software, r_1 can be automatically generated by the computer. If you are doing this manually, you can assign a random value to r_1. Since r_1 is a random number within the range [0, 1], there is a 90% probability that it falls within the interval [0, 0.9] and a 10% probability that it falls within the interval [0.9, 1]. If $r_1 \leq 0.9$, the two individuals will crossover; otherwise, they will not. Here, we assume that r_1 is 0.3, which is less than 0.9, so C and D will crossover.

One-point crossover is performed by randomly setting a cutting point in the individuals. In Fig. 5.6, the red dashed line represents the cutting point. Offspring can be produced in two ways. The first way is combining the genes on the left side of the cutting point in parent 1 with the genes on the right side of the cutting point in parent 2. The second way is combining the genes on the left side of the cutting point in parent 1 with the genes that remain in parent 2 after removing from parent 2 the genes on the left side of the cutting point in parent 1.

For this problem, the first way may lead to infeasible solutions because directly combining the genes on the left side in C with the genes on the right side in D results in 2321, a route where city 2 is visited twice whereas city 4 is not visited. This differs from the problem definition and hence is infeasible. Therefore, we use the second way and combine genes 2 and 3 on the left side in C with genes 4 and 1 in D, which are the genes that remain in D after removing genes 2 and 3 from D. The produced offspring is a new individual distinct from any individuals in the initial population. We name it E, and E will be in the next generation.

Please note that the genes in an offspring must be in the same order as those in one of its parents. In other words, do not change the order of genes when transferring them from C and D to E.

A common practice is to produce two children from two parents. In the case of crossover, the two children will become individuals in the next generation. In the case of not crossover, the two parents themselves will be individuals in the next generation.

For example, Fig. 5.7a, b illustrate two ways of creating two children from parents C and D. In the first way, the left side in C is transferred to child 1 and the left side in D is transferred to child 2 (Fig. 5.7a). In the second way, the left side in C is transferred to child 1, then a new cutting point is selected randomly and the new left side in C is transferred to child 2 (Fig. 5.7b).

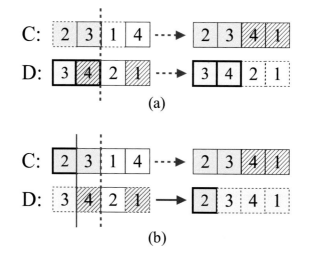

Fig. 5.7 An example of producing two children from two parents

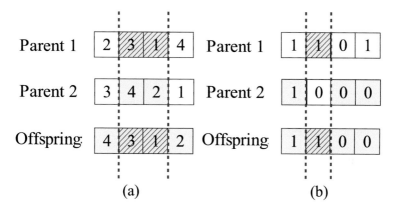

Fig. 5.8 An example of two-point crossover

In the case of two-point crossover, randomly select two cutting points and apply the same process as in one-point crossover. Figure 5.8a shows an example of applying two-point crossover to C and D, and Fig. 5.8b provides another example where the gene values are either 0 or 1.

5.3.5 Mutation

Mutation is an operator that mimics natural mutations in living organisms. For example, in nature, parents with blue eyes might have a child with black eyes due

Fig. 5.9 An example of
mutation by random gene
exchange

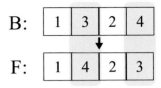

to a genetic mutation. In GA, mutation means some genes in an individual undergo change randomly, and hence the individual becomes a new one. Similar to mutation rates in nature, the mutation rate in GA is typically low, often ranging from 1 to 10%. The method for implementing the mutation rate is the same as that used for implementing the crossover rate.

To perform mutation, randomly pick up one individual and change the value of one or more genes, or randomly exchange two genes in it.

For example, we perform mutation through random gene exchange with a mutation rate of 10% to produce one individual from the initial population shown in Fig. 5.4. First, we randomly pick up one individual, which in this case is B. Next, we generate a random number r_2 in the range [0, 1]. If r_2 is no greater than 0.1, the individual will mutate, and the mutated individual will be in the next generation. If r_2 is greater than 0.1, the individual will remain unchanged and itself will be in the next generation. We assume that r_2 is 0.2, which is greater than 0.1, and hence B will not mutate but remain in the next generation.

In the case that r_2 is less than 0.1, B will mutate and Fig. 5.9 shows an example of it. We randomly choose the second and the fourth genes and exchange their values. The mutated individual is a new individual distinct from any individuals in the initial population, and we name it F.

5.3.6 Termination Criterion

When the termination criterion is met, stop producing the next generation and output the result. Usually, it takes hundreds or thousands of generations to find a high-quality solution to an NP-hard optimization problem.

Commonly used termination criteria include:

1. The number of generations has reached the set limit.
2. The execution time has reached the set limit.
3. The objective function value of the best individual found has not been updated for the set number of generations.

In the third criterion, "update" means that an individual with higher fitness than the best individual in the previous generation has been found. For example, consider the second generation in the above example: D, B, E, B. Among them, D and the first B are from selection, E is from crossover, and the last B is from mutation. The best individual is E, whose objective function value is 28. Since 28 is smaller than 29 (the objective function value of D, the best individual in the first generation), the objective function value of the best individual is updated. If the objective function value of E is 29, i.e. the same as that of D, then the objective function value is not updated.

When performing selection, crossover, and mutation, the selected or produced individuals may be the same as existing individuals in either the current generation or the next generation. In the above example, there are two Bs in the next generation. This is not a significant problem in GA, as it is similar to the existence of twins and very similar parent and child in human society. However, if the same individuals in one generation are large in number, it may have negative effect on exploring the optimal solution due to lack of diversity among the individuals.

When the termination criterion is satisfied, output the objective function value of the best individual in the final generation as the result. In the above example, if the procedure ends in the second generation, the objective function value of the best individual E, 28, will be the output. Typically, the objective function value is output, as it provides a straightforward indication of the quality of the best individual. If needed, the best individual can also be displayed.

Exercises
Single machine scheduling problem
　　Five jobs sharing a common due date will be processed on a single machine (Fig. 5.10). Find the sequence for processing the jobs so that the total deviation between each job's completion time and the due date is minimized.
　　Assumptions:

1. The first job is processed at time zero.
2. Once a job is finished, the next job will be processed immediately, with no idle time between jobs.

　　The mathematical model for this problem was previously provided in Sect. 4.3.1, and the encoding was shown in Fig. 4.5. Additionally, the following information is provided:
　　$d = 30$.
　　$P_1 = 5, P_2 = 10, P_3 = 15, P_4 = 20, P_5 = 25$.
　　Use GA to solve this problem by completing the following seven steps:

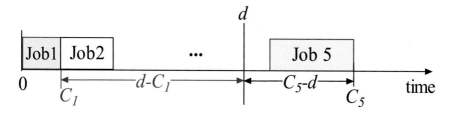

Fig. 5.10 Single machine scheduling problem for exercises

1. Initial population creation: create five individuals randomly.
2. Evaluation: calculate the objective function value for each individual and rank their fitness.
3. Selection: use elite selection to select one individual and tournament selection ($k = 3$) to select another (the two individuals can be the same).
4. Crossover: use an 80% crossover rate with one-point crossover to produce two children from the same two parents (randomly assign a value to the random number r_1, but perform crossover at least once).
5. Mutation: apply a 10% mutation rate with random gene exchange to produce one individual (randomly assign a value to the random number r_2, but perform mutation at least once).
6. Termination criterion: continue repeating the above steps until the objective function value of the best individual remains unchanged for one generation.
7. Result output: output the objective function value of the best individual found.

• Guidance

As an example, we create an individual shown in Fig. 5.11. The individual should consist of five jobs: job 1, job 2, job 3, job 4, and job 5. According to assumption 1, the first job, job 1, starts processing at time zero. According to assumption 2, there is no idle time between jobs.

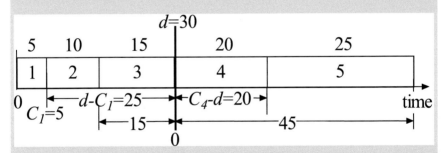

Fig. 5.11 An illustration of individual creation and evaluation

We show the given processing times for each job above them and depict the due date as a vertical line. Since the sum of the processing times for jobs 1, 2, and 3 is 30, the due date is equivalent to the completion time of job 3.

We proceed to calculate the objective function (Eq. 4.1 in Sect. 4.3.1) value for this individual. The objective function represents the sum of the deviations between each job's completion time and the due date.

For job 1, whose processing time is $P_1 = 5$, the start time is 0 and the completion time is $C_1 = 5$. With the due date being 30, the deviation is d - C_1 $= 30 - 5 = 25$. Alternatively, this deviation can be obtained by summing the processing times of job 2 (10) and job 3 (15), as their total duration equals the deviation between C_1 and d. For job 2, the deviation is 15, equivalent to the duration of job 3. For job 3, the deviation is 0 because $d - C_3 = 30 - 30 = 0$. For job 4, the deviation is 20, equivalent to the duration of job 4. For job 5, the deviation is 45, equivalent to the sum of the durations of jobs 4 and 5, i.e. $20 + 25 = 45$. The objective function value is the sum of all these deviations, totaling $25 + 15 + 0 + 20 + 45 = 105$.

For each individual created, you can obtain such an objective function value. Since there are five individuals in the initial population, you will have five such values. You can then compare these values to perform selection and proceed with the remaining steps in the exercises.

References

1. Mitchell M (1998) An introduction to genetic algorithms. MIT Press, Cambridge, Massachusetts, US
2. Obitko M (1998) Introduction to genetic algorithms. https://www.obitko.com/tutorials/genetic-algorithms/about.php

Chapter 6
Artificial Intelligence—Machine Learning

6.1 What is Machine Learning

Machine learning is a subfield of AI that seeks to replicate the learning capabilities of humans on computers. It has extensive applications in tasks such as object recognition, which involves recognizing and understanding input data to achieve intelligent processing. Some notable applications of machine learning include speech recognition, character recognition, image recognition, anomaly detection, medical diagnosis, financial market prediction, and obstacle sensing in self-driving technology.

Machine learning plays a crucial role in imitating the five human senses—sight, hearing, touch, taste, and smell—by processing perceptual information. For example, computer vision aims to replicate human vision and is often applied in the development of robotic eyes. It goes beyond mere image capture, encompassing tasks like extracting information from images and understanding scenes. Pattern recognition is a process of classifying patterns, such as speech and images, into distinct categories. The next level of pattern recognition is the understanding of patterns and scenes. Natural language processing enables computers to work with human language. It facilitates interaction between machines and humans, including tasks like speech recognition for text input, text-to-speech synthesis for information presentation, and predictive text input on smartphones and personal computers.

The process of machine learning is training a computer by inputting data samples and allowing the computer to derive valuable rules and criteria from these samples. Subsequently, the computer employs the extracted rules to make decisions when presented with new inputs.

© The Author(s), under exclusive license to Springer Nature Singapore Pte Ltd. 2024
W. Weng, *A Beginner's Guide to Informatics and Artificial Intelligence*,
https://doi.org/10.1007/978-981-97-1477-3_6

6.2 Types of Machine Learning

Machine learning can be broadly categorized into two main types: supervised learning and unsupervised learning. In supervised learning, the supervisor is not a human teacher but the correct output. The computer learns from data samples where each record is labeled the correct output. For example, input many images of cats and dogs labeled with their respective correct answers, i.e. a cat or a dog, into a computer and let the computer learn to recognize whether a newly input picture is a cat or a dog. In contrast, if the computer learns from data samples with no label of the correct output, it is called unsupervised learning.

Supervised learning includes various techniques, and among them, regression and classification are two fundamental techniques. Regression aims to predict numerical values for given inputs [1]. For example, consider Fig. 6.1a, which displays a set of records containing time and temperature data points. Each record, such as (t_1, T_1), represents the temperature T_1 at time t_1. Collectively, these records are referred to as data samples. When we input these data samples into a computer, their distribution is illustrated in Fig. 6.1b. The computer's task is to find a function that accurately represents the distribution or trend of these data. As shown in Fig. 6.1c, the computer may find a function like $T = kt + b$. This function can then be used to predict the temperature at a future time, such as temperature T_{n+1} at time t_{n+1}. Notably, t_{n+1} is a new input that was not present in the original data samples, and T_{n+1} is the predicted output based on the function.

Regression can also be applied to complex data distributions. For example, by inputting historical stock price movement data samples, a function that fits the movement, such as a sine or cosine function, can be discovered and used to predict future price movements.

Classification assigns attributes or types to input data. For example, if we categorize human facial expressions into joyful, angry, sad, and neutral, and train a computer

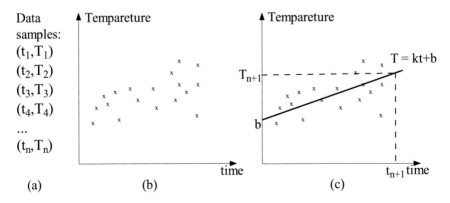

Fig. 6.1 An example of using regression for prediction

with labeled data samples of numerous facial expressions, it can subsequently classify new facial expressions into one of these types. Classification that can return one of two types is used for tasks like detecting harmful or harmless bacteria, assessing the normalcy or abnormality of a machine, identifying ordinary or spam emails, and determining whether a program is harmless or a virus.

Unsupervised learning does not rely on correct answers and allows a computer to learn automatically from vast datasets by extracting structure, patterns, and rules. One unsupervised learning technique is clustering, which groups input data.

In addition to regression and classification, machine learning encompasses various techniques, including decision tree learning, relational rule learning, reinforcement learning, and neural network. These techniques are not limited to supervised learning or a single type of learning. In this textbook, we will focus on neural network, which has gained significant attention in recent years, especially with the rise of deep learning.

6.3 Neural Network

6.3.1 What is a Neural Network

A neural network, also known as an artificial neural network, is a computational model inspired by the neural network that makes up the human brain. It is composed of multiple artificial neurons connected by synapses. By adjusting the strength of synaptic connections through a learning process, a neural network can be employed to solve a wide range of problems.

Figure 6.2 illustrates a simplified neural network, with each circle representing a neuron and the arrows representing synapses [2]. The direction of an arrow represents the flow of information. A neural network consists of three primary layers: the input layer, the output layer, and optional hidden layers. The hidden layers are termed as such because they remain invisible from the user, who can observe only the input and output. Each layer must contain at least one neuron, and each neuron should be connected to all the neurons in the subsequent layer. The strength of connections is known as synaptic strength and may differ among synapses.

A neuron, often referred to as a node or unit, receives information from the input layer or other neurons. The most commonly used model for a neuron is Eq. 6.1 [1].

$$y = f\left(\sum_{i=1}^{n} w_i x_i - \theta\right) \tag{6.1}$$

In this equation, y represents the output, and x_i represents the ith input. For example, consider the neuron in the output layer illustrated in Fig. 6.2. It has three inputs: x_1, x_2, and x_3. Each input has a weight w_i, representing its synaptic strength. In other words, w_1 is the weight of x_1, w_2 is the weight of x_2, and w_3 is the weight of x_3. The weighted sum of these inputs is denoted as $\sum_i w_i x_i$. This sum is compared with

Hidden layers

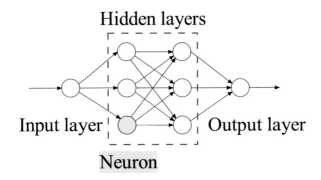

Input layer   Output layer

Neuron

Fig. 6.2 A simple neural network

a threshold value θ of the neuron. If the weighted sum is no less than the threshold, the neuron will become excited, resulting in an increase in the output value y. In the following, we will provide detailed explanations using the threshold logic unit as an illustrative example.

6.3.2 Threshold Logic Unit (TLU)

The threshold logic unit (TLU), depicted in Fig. 6.3, is a single neuron having n inputs x_1 to x_n and one output y. If the weighted sum of inputs $\sum_{i=1}^{n} w_i x_i$ is less than the threshold, the output will be 0. If the weighted sum of inputs $\sum_{i=1}^{n} w_i x_i$ is greater than or equal to the threshold, the output will be 1 (Eq. 6.2) [3].

$$
y = \begin{cases} 0, & \text{if } \sum_{i=1}^{n} w_i x_i < \theta, \\ 1, & \text{if } \sum_{i=1}^{n} w_i x_i \geq \theta. \end{cases}
\tag{6.2}
$$

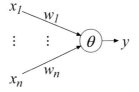

Fig. 6.3 Threshold logic unit

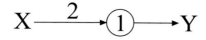

Fig. 6.4 A TLU with a single input

Table 6.1 Truth table of the TLU in Fig. 6.4

Input	Output
X	Y
0	0
1	1

Figure 6.4 shows a TLU with a threshold of 1 and a single input X whose weight is 2. Table 6.1 presents the truth table of this TLU. Let us explain why the output values Y are 0 for $X = 0$ and 1 for $X = 1$, respectively.

When $X = 0$, the weighted sum of inputs is $wX = 2 \times 0 = 0$. Compared with the threshold 1, the weighted sum is less. According to the model function Eq. 6.2, when the weighted sum is less than the threshold value, the output Y will be 0.

When $X = 1$, the weighted sum becomes $wX = 2 \times 1 = 2$. Compared with the threshold 1, the weighted sum is greater. According to the model function, when the weighted sum is greater than or equal to the threshold value, the output Y will be 1.

When the weight w and threshold θ are modified to 1 and 2, respectively, as illustrated in Fig. 6.5, the truth table transforms into Table 6.2. When the input is 0, the weighted sum is $1 \times 0 = 0$. Compared with the threshold 2, the weighted sum is less. According to the model function, if the weighted sum is less than the threshold, the output Y will be 0. When the input is 1, the weighted sum is $1 \times 1 = 1$, still less than the threshold 2. According to the model function, the output Y will be 0.

Comparing the neurons in Figs. 6.4 and 6.5, it can be observed that only the weight and threshold values differ. In summary, altering the synaptic strength (weights and threshold) of a neuron leads to a change in the output for the same input.

Table 6.2 Truth table of the TLU in Fig. 6.5

Input	Output
X	Y
0	0
1	0

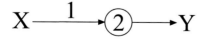

Fig. 6.5 Another TLU with a single input

• **Questions**

1. Can a TLU with a single input (Fig. 6.6) produce an output of 1 for both X = 0 and X = 1? In other words, can the truth table of a TLU be Table 6.3? If possible, please give an example of the weight w and threshold θ values that would achieve this.

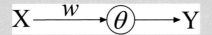

Fig. 6.6 TLU for questions 1 and 2

Table 6.3 Truth table for question 1

Input	Output
X	Y
0	1
1	1

Hint: when X = 0, the weighted sum is $w \times 0 = 0$. According to the model function Eq. 6.2, if $0 \geq \theta$, the output Y will be 1. When X = 1, the weighted sum is $w \times 1 = w$, and if $w \geq \theta$, the output Y will be 1. Therefore, the question can be rephrased as "Are there values of w and θ that can satisfy both $0 \geq \theta$ and $w \geq \theta$?" If so, please give an example of the values for w and θ.

2. Can a TLU with a single input (Fig. 6.6) produce an output of 1 for X = 0 and an output of 0 for X = 1? In other words, can the truth table of a TLU be Table 6.4? If possible, please give an example of the weight w and threshold θ values that would achieve this.

Table 6.4 Truth table for question 2

Input	Output
X	Y
0	1
1	0

Hint: Similar to question 1, if there are values of w and θ that satisfy both conditions $0 \geq \theta$ and $w < \theta$, it will be possible to output 1 and 0 for inputs 1 and 0, respectively. Consider if such values exist.

As shown in Figs. 6.5 and 6.6 and the above questions, the output of a neuron can vary for the same input if the weights and threshold values change. This ability

Fig. 6.7 A TLU with the same number of inputs as logic gate OR

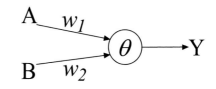

Table 6.5 Truth table of the logic OR operation

Input		Output
A	B	T
0	0	0
0	1	1
1	0	1
1	1	1

to produce different outputs for the same input is a fundamental feature of neural network. This feature can be used to implement various functions.

Next, we provide an example of using a TLU to imitate the logic gate OR, one of the basic logic gates introduced in Sect. 1.7. This means we will demonstrate how to configure the weights and threshold of a TLU to produce the same results as the logic OR operation.

First, create a TLU with two inputs as shown in Fig. 6.7, because the logic gate OR has two inputs.

Second, set the weights w_1, w_2, and threshold θ of the TLU to match the output of logic gate OR. The value-setting process includes three steps.

Step 1: create the truth table for the inputs and the correct outputs of the logic OR operation, as presented in Table 6.5. In this table, the inputs are A and B, and the output is T. When at least one input is one, the output will be one. Only when both inputs are zero will the output be zero.

Step 2: create a constraint for each of the four input patterns. For the input pattern $A = 0$ and $B = 0$, the weighted sum of inputs is $w_1 \times 0 + w_2 \times 0$. According to the model function Eq. 6.2, if this sum is less than θ, the output will be 0, matching the correct output (T column in Table 6.5). Therefore, the constraint is $w_1 \times 0 + w_2 \times 0 < \theta$. In other words, we need to set the values of w_1, w_2, and θ to satisfy $w_1 \times 0 + w_2 \times 1 < \theta$ so that the TLU's output aligns with the logic OR output for this input pattern.

Similarly, for the input pattern $A = 0$ and $B = 1$, the weighted sum of inputs is $w_1 \times 0 + w_2 \times 1$. According to the model function, if this sum is greater than or equal to θ, the output will be 1, matching the correct output. Therefore, the constraint is $w_1 \times 0 + w_2 \times 1 \geq \theta$. In other words, we need to set the values of w_1, w_2, and θ to satisfy $w_1 \times 0 + w_2 \times 1 \geq \theta$ so that the TLU's output aligns with the logic OR output for this input pattern.

In summary, when the correct output is 0, the weighted sum should be less than θ, and when the correct output is 1, the weighted sum should be greater than or equal to to θ. The resulting four constraints are shown in Eqs. 6.3–6.6. Equations 6.7–6.10 are the calculation results, such as $w_1 \times 0 + w_2 \times 0 = 0$ and $w_1 \times 0 + w_2 \times 1 = w_2$.

$$w_1 \times 0 + w_2 \times 0 < \theta \qquad (6.3)$$

$$w_1 \times 0 + w_2 \times 1 \geq \theta \qquad (6.4)$$

$$w_1 \times 1 + w_2 \times 0 \geq \theta \qquad (6.5)$$

$$w_1 \times 1 + w_2 \times 1 \geq \theta \qquad (6.6)$$

$$0 < \theta \qquad (6.7)$$

$$w_2 \geq \theta \qquad (6.8)$$

$$w_1 \geq \theta \qquad (6.9)$$

$$w_1 + w_2 \geq \theta \qquad (6.10)$$

Step 3: determine the values for w_i and θ that satisfy all the constraints. Since both w_i and θ are real numbers, numerous combinations can satisfy the four constraints. For example, $w_1 = 2$, $w_2 = 2$, $\theta = 1$; $w_1 = 2.4$, $w_2 = 1.7$, $\theta = 0.6$; and $w_1 = 15.7$, $w_2 = 159$, $\theta = 0.02$.

After setting values for the weights and threshold, it is recommended to verify the TLU's actual output. For example, for a TLU with $w_1 = 2$, $w_2 = 2$, and $\theta = 1$ (as shown in Fig. 6.8), you can calculate its actual output using Eqs. 6.11–6.14. When $A = 0$ and $B = 0$, the weighted sum of inputs is $0 \times 2 + 0 \times 2 = 0$, which is less than the threshold 1, resulting in an output of 0. If all four actual outputs match the values in the T (target) column in Table 6.5, it is confirmed that the weights and threshold have been set correctly.

$$A = 0, B = 0 \rightarrow 0 \times 2 + 0 \times 2 = 0 < 1 \rightarrow Y = 0 \qquad (6.11)$$

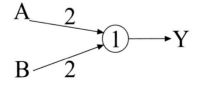

Fig. 6.8 A TLU with $w_1 = 2$, $w_2 = 2$, and $\theta = 1$

$$A = 0, B = 1 \rightarrow 0 \times 2 + 1 \times 2 = 2 \geq 1 \rightarrow Y = 1 \quad (6.12)$$

$$A = 1, B = 0 \rightarrow 1 \times 2 + 0 \times 2 = 2 \geq 1 \rightarrow Y = 1 \quad (6.13)$$

$$A = 1, B = 1 \rightarrow 1 \times 2 + 1 \times 2 = 4 \geq 1 \rightarrow Y = 1 \quad (6.14)$$

Besides the logic OR operation, a single TLU can be employed to implement various logic operations, including the logic AND and combinations of logic circuits. Several examples will be given in the exercises.

6.3.3 Learning of TLU

The purpose of neural network learning is to enable a computer to automatically set the weights and thresholds for each neuron. For a TLU, the values to be set are w_1 to w_n and θ. During TLU learning, the input vector is $(x_1, x_2, ..., x_n)$, the correct output is t (target), and the actual output is y. If $y \neq t$, the weight vector $(w_1, w_2, ..., w_n)$ and θ will be updated as follows [4].

$$\forall i \in \{1, ..., n\} : \begin{cases} \theta^{(new)} = \theta^{(old)} + \Delta\theta, & \Delta\theta = -\eta(t - y) \\ w_i^{(new)} = w_i^{(old)} + \Delta w_i, & \Delta w_i = \eta(t - y)x_i \end{cases} \quad (6.15)$$

If the actual output y differs from the correct output t, $\Delta\theta$ will be calculated as the difference between y and t multiplied by a learning coefficient η. The new θ value is obtained by adding $\Delta\theta$ to the old θ value. Similarly, let $\Delta w_i = \eta(t - y)x_i$, the new w_i value is obtained by adding Δw_i to the old w_i value. These updates to θ and w_i will continue until $y = t$.

The learning coefficient η is in the range of $(0, 1)$. When η approaches 0, the updates have smaller magnitudes, resulting in slower learning. Conversely, as η approaches 1, the updates become larger, potentially leading to faster learning. However, it is essential to note that increasing η indiscriminately does not necessarily accelerate learning. This is because overly large updates may hinder convergence of y toward the target t, especially when dealing with complex functions.

To illustrate this, consider the case where y is represented by a curve depicted in Fig. 6.9, and t is its lowest point. If the learning coefficient is set too high, the model may skip over many values during each iteration, making it challenging to reach t accurately. Therefore, selecting an appropriate value for η is crucial and should strike a balance between rapid learning and convergence to the desired output.

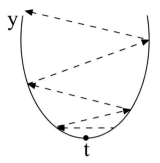

Fig. 6.9 An example of radical updates of y

• **Questions**

3. Which type of learning does the learning of a TLU belong to?

    A. Supervised learning
    B. Unsupervised learning

Hint: consider if the learning of a TLU needs the correct output or not.

The learning process of a TLU will update the weights (w_1, w_2,…, w_n) and threshold θ until the actual output y becomes the same as the correct output t. It is important to note that not all problems can be effectively solved using a single TLU. For example, in cases where there are no combinations of weights w_i and threshold θ values that can satisfy all the constraints, such as those illustrated in Eqs. 6.16–6.19, the TLU's learning process may never converge to a solution.

$$0 < \theta \tag{6.16}$$

$$w_2 \geq \theta \tag{6.17}$$

$$w_1 \geq \theta \tag{6.18}$$

$$w_1 + w_2 < \theta \tag{6.19}$$

To address such problems, it becomes necessary to use a neural network with multiple neurons, and even hidden layers. In the upcoming section, we will provide a brief introduction to deep learning, which is a type of neural network characterized by its multilayered architecture.

6.3.4 Deep Learning

Deep learning is a problem-solving approach that uses large-scale hierarchical neural networks with multiple hidden layers.

Figure 6.10 illustrates the architecture of a deep learning neural network. A distinguishing characteristic of deep learning is that it is performed on neural networks with multiple (more than one) hidden layers. In other words, neural networks with zero (e.g. a TLU) or one hidden layer are commonly referred to as shallow networks rather than deep learning networks. Deep learning neural networks, as opposed to those with fewer hidden layers, exhibit superior capabilities in achieving higher accuracy in tasks like image and pattern recognition.

Deep learning offers several advantages, primarily stemming from its ability to handle complex data processing tasks when a sufficient amount of training data is available. With an ample dataset for training, a well-trained neural network can tackle tasks that are often too intricate for traditional machine learning algorithms. Furthermore, the accuracy of the trained neural network tends to increase proportionally with the quantity of training data.

On the downside, deep learning has its limitations. When the amount of training data is insufficient or when access to high-performance computing resources is lacking, deep learning may struggle to achieve high performance or become infeasible.

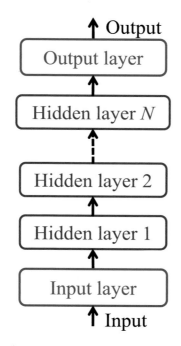

Fig. 6.10 Structure of a deep learning neural network

The most commonly used deep learning neural networks are Convolutional Neural Networks (CNNs) and Recurrent Neural Networks (RNNs).

CNNs are forward-propagating neural networks that excel at extracting local information and exhibiting location universality. Two-dimensional CNNs share structural similarities with neurons in the human visual cortex, which makes them particularly adept at pattern recognition. Figure 6.11 illustrates the architecture of a CNN used for image recognition.

The left part of a CNN, known as the feature extraction component, takes input images of various sizes and extracts features from them. This is performed using filters (also known as kernels) that are smaller than the input image. The filters act like windows, examining the image part by part as they traverse over the image (as shown in Fig. 6.12). On the right side, the classification component uses the extracted features to make predictions or determine the content of the image, outputting the final result. If you are interested in delving deeper into image recognition using CNNs, please refer to the reference [5].

RNNs are bidirectional neural networks that incorporate a recursive structure in its middle layers, where some of the outputs are used as inputs, as illustrated in Fig. 6.13. RNNs are well-suited for managing variable-length data, including audio

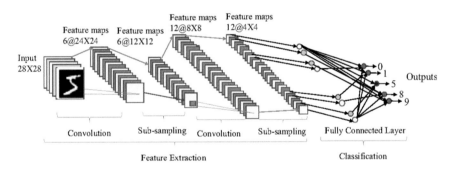

Fig. 6.11 Structure of a CNN used for image recognition

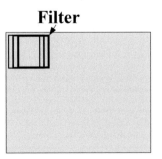

Fig. 6.12 A filter moving over an image

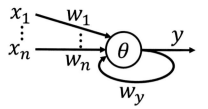

Fig. 6.13 Bidirectional propagation in an RNN

and video, and they excel in tasks such as speech recognition, video recognition, and natural language processing.

Exercises

1. Use a TLU to implement the logic calculation X_1 AND X_2 AND X_3.

• **Guidance**

Figure 6.14 illustrates the TLU for this problem. You need to specify the values for w_1, w_2, w_3, and θ.

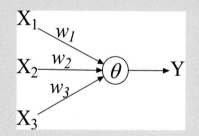

Fig. 6.14 A TLU with three inputs

First, create the truth table for the logic operation X_1 AND X_2 AND X_3. The truth table for the logic AND operation was previously provided and explained in Chap. 1. In case you need a refresher, please review it.

Table 6.6 is an example of a truth table with three inputs, X_1, X_2, and X_3. Each input has a value of either 0 or 1, resulting in a total of $2^3 = 8$ possible combinations. Please fill in the empty cells with the appropriate values.

Table 6.6 Truth table to complete for exercise problem 1

Input			Output
X_1	X_2	X_3	T

Once you have completed the truth table, proceed to derive a constraint based on the information in each row, following the examples provided in Sect. 6.3.2. Finally, set the values of w_1, w_2, w_3, and θ to ensure that all the eight constraints are satisfied.

2. Use a TLU to produce the output of the circuit shown in Fig. 6.15.

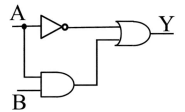

Fig. 6.15 Circuit for exercise problem 2

• **Guidance**
Similar to problem 1, start by creating the truth table for the circuit. This table should have two inputs, A and B, and one output. Since both A and B can be either 0 or 1, the table will consist of $2^2 = 4$ rows.

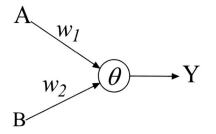

Fig. 6.16 A TLU for exercise problem 2

After completing the truth table, create a constraint based on the information in each row. Finally, set the values of the weights and threshold in such a way that all the four constraints are satisfied.

If you need a visual representation of the TLU for this circuit, refer to Fig. 6.16. It depicts a TLU with inputs A and B, and only one neuron is enough. You should specify the values of w_1, w_2, and θ. Since a single neuron can produce the output for this circuit, there is no need to create additional neurons.

3. According to the content of this textbook, what is the relation between the three fields: artificial intelligence (AI), machine learning (ML), and neural network (NN)?

• **Guidance**

If we use three circles to represent the three fields, as shown in Fig. 6.17, then Fig. 6.18 indicates partial overlap between two fields, and Fig. 6.19 indicates one field entirely encompassing another. You can illustrate the relation between the three fields using such visual expressions.

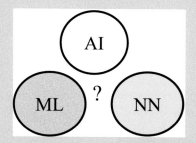

Fig. 6.17 Diagram for exercise problem 3

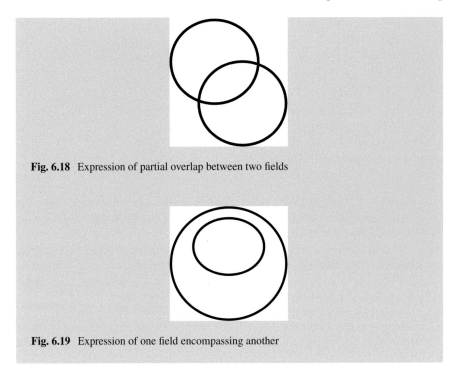

Fig. 6.18   Expression of partial overlap between two fields

Fig. 6.19   Expression of one field encompassing another

*4.   Use a TLU to implement the logic operation X_1 AND (X_2 OR X_3).
*5.   Please explain why a TLU cannot produce the output shown in Table 6.7.

Table 6.7   Truth table for exercise problem 5

Input			Output
X_1	X_2	X_3	T
0	0	0	0
0	0	1	1
0	1	0	1
0	1	1	1
1	0	0	1
1	0	1	1
1	1	0	1
1	1	1	0

References

1. Kruse R, Borgelt C, Braune C, Mostaghim S (2016) Introduction to neural networks. In: Computational intelligence. Texts in computer science. Springer, London. https://doi.org/10.1007/978-1-4471-7296-3_2
2. Orr G, Schraudolph N, Cummins F (1999) Lecture notes of neural networks. https://willamette.edu/~gorr/classes/cs449/intro.html
3. Blais A, Mertz D (2001) An introduction to neural networks—pattern learning with back propagation algorithm. Gnosis Software, Inc. https://www.sci.brooklyn.cuny.edu/~sklar/teaching/s06/ai/papers/nn-intro.pdf
4. Stergiou C, Siganos D (2011) Neural networks. https://wiki.eecs.yorku.ca/course_archive/2011-12/F/4403/_media/report.pdf
5. Ujjwalkarn (2016) An intuitive explanation of convolutional neural networks. https://ujjwalkarn.me/2016/08/11/intuitive-explanation-convnets/

Chapter 7
Network

7.1 What is a Network

A network refers to connections between nodes, where each node represents an element or thing. There are various types of networks, including information networks, railway networks, and logistics networks. An information network consists of multiple information devices like telephones and computers connected by communication channels. While the terms "network" and "information network" are not identical, "network" often refers to an information network in many contexts. In this textbook, unless otherwise stated, the term "network" specifically refers to information network.

7.2 Methods of Switching

Information networks can be categorized based on their switching methods [1]. There are two main types: circuit-switched networks, represented by the telephone network, and packet-switched networks, represented by computer networks. In the following, we will provide detailed explanations of each type.

In a telephone network, each telephone is connected to a cable, which is, in turn, connected to an exchange station (see Fig. 7.1). The number of cables between an exchange station and a relay station might be less than the cables between the exchange station and telephone terminals. Consequently, the simultaneous usage of telephones may be limited by the availability of cables between the exchange station and the relay station.

Since each terminal exclusively uses a cable, a circuit-switched network is ideal for transmitting continuous information like voice. However, the limited number of cables restricts the simultaneous use of terminals.

© The Author(s), under exclusive license to Springer Nature Singapore Pte Ltd. 2024   69
W. Weng, *A Beginner's Guide to Informatics and Artificial Intelligence*,
https://doi.org/10.1007/978-981-97-1477-3_7

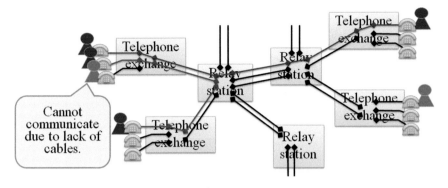

Fig. 7.1 Circuit-switched network

Unlike circuit-switched networks that primarily handle continuous data like voice, computer networks transmit a variety of data types. Using a switching system where each communication exclusively occupies a cable would result in low efficiency. Therefore, computer networks use a packet-switched system, where data is divided into fixed-size packets. In a packet-switched network, multiple communications can share a cable simultaneously, allowing for a high degree of concurrent communication.

In Fig. 7.2, each host represents a personal computer (PC) user. Communication data from user A to user B passes through three routers before reaching user B, while communication data from user C to user D traverses four routers before reaching user D. The cable connecting the central router and the upper-right router is shared by both communications. Packets from A to B are shown in brown, and packets from C to D are shown in yellow.

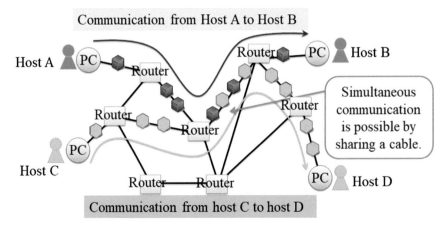

Fig. 7.2 Packet-switched network

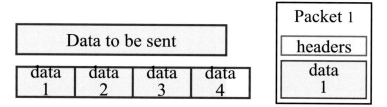

Fig. 7.3 Relation between data to be sent and a packet

Figure 7.3 illustrates the relation between data to be sent and a packet in a packet-switched network. The data is divided into the packet size, which is smaller than the data size [1]. Each packet consists of a portion of the data and headers containing information to identify the data, including sender, destination, type, serial number, and size. A detailed explanation of header structure will be provided in Sect. 7.5.1.

7.3 Network Topologies

Network topologies define the network's connection type or configuration. In the early days, when computers were expensive, networks were developed to allow multiple terminals to share a single computer. The predominant topology at that time was the star topology, known for its efficient cable usage but vulnerable to network-wide failure if the central device malfunctions.

Other network topologies include bus, line, ring, tree, and mesh types. Bus topology was common in early Ethernets. Line topology suits smaller systems but is vulnerable to network-wide failure if any device malfunctions. Ring topology offers redundancy with minimal cables. Table 7.1 provides a summary of different network topologies along with their respective characteristics. The selection of a network topology should align with the specific type and intended purpose of the network.

7.4 Physical Configuration

Based on the physical configuration, networks can be categorized into two main types: wired local area network (LAN) and wireless LAN.

7.4.1 Wired LAN (Ethernet)

A wired LAN is commonly referred to as Ethernet [1]. Ethernet standards consist of three components, as depicted in Fig. 7.4: the number on the left side indicates the

Table 7.1 Network topologies

Type	Characteristics	
Star	A network configuration where multiple devices are connected to a central hub or switch. It offers efficient cable usage. If a cable fails, only one node is affected. However, a central device failure can bring down the entire network	
Bus	A network configuration where multiple devices are connected to a single shared bus, with terminators at both ends to prevent signal reflection and noise. This configuration was prevalent in the early days of Ethernet	
Line	A network configuration where multiple devices are connected in a linear series. This configuration is simple, but if any of the devices experiences a failure or goes offline, it can disrupt the entire network's functionality	
Ring	A network configuration where device connections create a circular data path. Each networked device is connected to two others, forming a circular data path resembling points on a circle. One advantage of this configuration is that it allows for cable redundancy while minimizing the number of cables required	
Tree	A network configuration where connected devices are arranged like the branches of a tree	
Mesh	A network configuration where each device is interconnected with every other device. This configuration ensures maximum transmission reliability, even if one connection fails. However, it requires a significant number of cables due to its high redundancy	

Fig. 7.4 An example of
Ethernet standards

$$
\begin{pmatrix} 10 \\ 100 \\ 1000 \\ 10G \end{pmatrix} Base \begin{pmatrix} 2 \\ 5 \\ T \\ TX \\ FX \\ etc \end{pmatrix}
$$

maximum data rate, "Base" or "Fast" in the middle refers to the signaling type, and the number or letters on the right side denote the type of cable used. For example, in the "10BASE-T" standard, "10" indicates a maximum data rate of 10 Mbps (10 million bits per second); "Base" signifies the use of baseband signaling, and "T" means the network is wired using twisted pair copper cables.

Notably, Fig. 7.4 is an example of Ethernet standards. The figure does not include all Ethernet standards, and not all data rates on the left side can be paired with the numbers or letters on the right side.

In an Ethernet standard, the key element is the "maximum data rate" on the left side. Currently, Ethernet networks with a maximum data rate of only 10 Mbps are uncommon. Most Ethernet networks offer a maximum data rate of 100 Mbps or 1000 Mbps. While Ethernet networks with a maximum data rate of 10 Gbps (10,000 Mbps) are available, they are not yet widely adopted.

Ethernet connections can be established using either copper cabling or fiber optic cabling. In a copper cabling Ethernet, data is transmitted through copper cables. Previously, ADSL was primarily used for broadband Internet access over traditional copper telephone lines. It offers a maximum downstream (download) data rate of up to 24 Mbps. Upstream (upload) speeds are lower than downstream speeds. One advantage of ADSL is its ability to carry both voice communication (telephone service) and data communication (Internet service) over the same copper cable simultaneously. This is achieved by using different frequency bands for voice and data, allowing both services to coexist without interference. However, ADSL has been largely replaced by faster and more capable broadband technologies. Currently, one of the most prevalent forms of copper cabling Ethernet is twisted pair cabling Ethernet including Fast Ethernet (100 Mbps) and Gigabit Ethernet (1 Gbps).

Copper cabling has its drawbacks, including vulnerability to interference, lower quality for voice communication, and decrease in data rate as the distance from the closest exchange station increases. For example, an ADSL Ethernet may achieve the maximum data rate when the customer's location is within 100 m of the nearest exchange station. As the distance from the exchange station increases, the data rate gradually decreases due to signal attenuation and other factors. Beyond a certain distance, the achievable data rate may significantly decrease.

In contrast, fiber optic cabling Ethernet offers distinct advantages, including high data rates over long distances. This technology relies on optical fibers for data transmission. With a maximum data rate exceeding 10 Gbps and a reach of over 40 km, fiber optics excel in providing high-speed connectivity over considerable distances. They are also known for their resilience against external interference, even in challenging environments with high levels of noise. However, fiber optic cables are vulnerable to physical damage, including scratches, bends, and stains. If the optical fibers suffer from such issues, it can lead to a sudden network outage.

7.4.2 Wireless LAN (Wi-Fi)

Wireless LANs, also known as Wi-Fi, are standardized by IEEE 802.11 [1, 2]. Their standards have gone through multiple iterations and revisions. At present, the most commonly known ones among the IEEE 802.11 family include IEEE 802.11a, IEEE 802.11b, IEEE 802.11g, IEEE 802.11n, IEEE 802.11ac, and IEEE 802.11ax.

Table 7.2 displays the frequency bands, maximum data rates, and characteristics of these Wi-Fi standards. For example, the 802.11a Wi-Fi operates in the 5 GHz frequency band and offers a maximum data rate of 54 Mbps. It is unlikely to be interfered by electronic devices like microwave ovens and Bluetooth devices, but has limited ability to go through obstacles.

Comparing the Wi-Fi standards listed in Table 7.2 with the Ethernet standards shown in Fig. 7.4, it can be known that Wi-Fi can match or even surpass Ethernet in terms of data speed. For example, the maximum data rate of an 802.11ax Wi-Fi reaches 9.6 Gbps, significantly faster than many common Ethernet standards with maximum rates of 100 Mbps or 1 Gbps.

Table 7.2 Details of commonly known IEEE802.11 standards

x	Frequency band	Maximum data rate	Characteristics	
			Likelihood to be interfered	Ability to go through obstacles
a	5 GHz	54 Mbps	Low	Weak
b	2.4 GHz	11 Mbps	High	Strong
g	2.4 GHz	54 Mbps	High	Strong
n	2.4 GHz	600 Mbps	High	Strong
	5 GHz	600 Mbps	Low	Weak
ac	5 GHz	6.9 Gbps	Low	Weak
ax	2.4 GHz	9.6 Gbps	High	Strong
	5 GHz	9.6 Gbps	Low	Weak

• Questions

1. According to the details of the Wi-Fi standards in Table 7.2, which item determines the characteristics of a Wi-Fi network?

7.5 Internet

In a broad sense, the term "Internet" refers to a network in which multiple networks are interconnected. However, when we use the term "Internet" in a narrow sense, we are typically referring to the vast global-scale interconnected network that originated from ARPANET, a military network of the US Department of Defense. ARPANET was designed to withstand damage and continue functioning even if parts of it were destroyed. Today, when we say "the Internet", we are usually referring to this global network, which is much more extensive and widely used than a generic "internet".

7.5.1 Internet Protocols

A communication protocol is a set of predetermined rules for transmitting and processing information. It serves as the essential framework for ensuring correct information exchange between senders and receivers. It is similar to sending a postal letter, where one must write the recipient's address, place the letter in an envelope, and affix a stamp.

For information communication on the Internet, a great number of protocols are needed. These include protocols for the cables connecting devices and protocols for processing different types of data, such as text, voice, and images. If only one protocol is used as a single system to meet all these needs, it can be imagined that this single protocol would become very large in scale and, consequently, difficult to maintain. Therefore, a hierarchical model is employed to facilitate the development and modification of protocols.

There are two hierarchical models of protocols. One is the Open Systems Interconnection (OSI) model developed by the International Organization for Standardization (ISO), and the other is the TCP/IP model, which is currently in use [2]. The term "TCP/IP" collectively refers to the two most widely used protocols: TCP, which stands for Transmission Control Protocol, and IP, which stands for Internet Protocol.

Table 7.3 provides a comparison of the two models. The OSI model comprises 7 layers, which are, from layer 1 to layer 7: the physical layer, data link layer, network layer, transport layer, session layer, presentation layer, and application layer. This model is not intended for practical implementation and is referred to as a reference model. It serves as a foundation for the development of multilayered protocols

Table 7.3 OSI model versus TCP/IP model

OSI model	TCP/IP model
Application layer (Layer 7) Provides communication function for applications	**Application layer (Layer 4)** Provides services to the application being used by the user
Presentation layer (Layer 6) Unifies formats of data expression	
Session layer (Layer 5) Manages data sequence	
Transport layer (Layer 4) Achieves reliable data transmission	**Transport layer (Layer 3)** Ensures reliability in data transmission
Network layer (Layer 3) Determines the transmission route and destination of data	**Internet layer (Layer 2)** Provides end-to-end data transmission
Data link layer (Layer 2) Controls data transmission to neighboring devices	**Network interface layer (Layer 1)** Provides methods of data transmission in the physical parts of a network
Physical layer (Layer 1) Provides methods of transmission in electronic and mechanical parts	

The TCP/IP model is currently in use and consists of 4 layers. In the model, layers 1 and 2 in the OSI reference model are combined into layer 1, known as the network interface layer, and layers 5 to 7 in the OSI reference model are combined into layer 4, known as the application layer.

Table 7.4 provides a list of widely used protocols in each layer of the TCP/IP model. In the network interface layer, protocols for Ethernet standards and Wi-Fi standards introduced in Sect. 7.4 are used. In the transport layer and the Internet layer, TCP and IP are used, respectively. In the application layer, HTTP is used for viewing web pages, and SMTP and POP are used for sending and receiving emails

Table 7.4 Examples of protocols in TCP/IP model

TCP/IP model	Examples of protocols
Application layer Provides services according to the application being used by the user	• Web: HTTP • E-mail: SMTP, POP, IMAP
Transport layer Ensures reliability in data transmission	TCP, UDP, ICMP
Internet layer Provides end-to-end data transmission	IP
Network interface layer Provides methods of data transmission in the physical parts of a network	• Ethernet:10/100/1000 Base-T/ FX • Wi-Fi: IEEE 802.11a/b/g/n/ac/ax

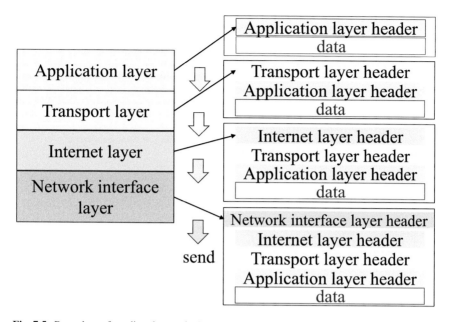

Fig. 7.5 Procedure of sending data to the Internet in TCP/IP model

In the TCP/IP model, data intended for transmission over the Internet flow downward from the upper layers to the lower layers. Initially, data is sent to the topmost layer, which then appends a layer header to the data before passing it down to the next lower layer. Each successive layer follows this process, receiving data from the layer above, adding its own layer header, and forwarding the modified data to the layer below. Finally, the data destined for Internet transmission contains four headers, each added by one of the layers, as illustrated in Fig. 7.5.

Accordingly, the headers in the packet introduced in Sect. 7.2 (Fig. 7.3) consist of headers from the application layer, transport layer, Internet layer, and network interface layer.

In contrast, data received from the Internet moves upward from lower layers to upper layers. Initially, the data is received by the lowest layer, which checks whether the data is addressed to it. If it is, the layer removes its own header from the data and then forwards the data to the layer above. Each subsequent layer follows this process, receiving data from the layer below, checking for addressing, and, if correct, removing its own layer header before forwarding the data to the layer above. Ultimately, the processed data contains no headers, as depicted in Fig. 7.6.

When verifying the destination of data, each layer employs a specific type of address. Among these addresses, the IP address used in the Internet layer is the most well-known. Aside from its role in transmitting and receiving data within the Internet layer, IP addresses are widely used for various other purposes.

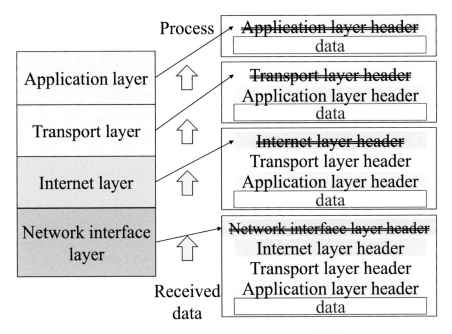

Fig. 7.6 Procedure of processing data received from the Internet in TCP/IP model

7.5.2 IP Address

An IP address serves as an identifier for a unique terminal connected to the Internet. Figure 7.7 illustrates an IP address, where 133.28.10.100 represents the IP address itself, and 80 is the port number. Typically, the port number is used to identify the software or application. For example, port number 80 is commonly associated with web browsers.

The range of IP addresses allocated to each country and region worldwide is pre-established and remains constant. For example, the IP addresses allocated for Kanazawa University start from 133.28.xx.xx [3]. Similarly, the IP address ranges for individual buildings and departments are also predetermined and fixed [3]. In other words, there is a direct correlation between an IP address and a location. As a result, if you know the IP address of a terminal device, you can know its location.

IP addresses can be divided into two categories: global addresses and private addresses. A global address is unique worldwide and does not duplicate anywhere else in the world. For example, the IP address shown in Fig. 7.7 is a global address. On the other hand, a private address is managed independently within an internal

Fig. 7.7 An example of IP address and port number

$$\boxed{133.28.10.100 \vdots 80}$$

IP address Port number

network, such as a company's or a home network. Private addresses typically begin with either "10." or "192.168."

There are two versions of IP addresses: IPv4 (Internet Protocol version 4) and IPv6 (Internet Protocol version 6). IPv4 has been in use since the early days of the Internet, while IPv6 was developed as the next-generation protocol. IPv4 uses a 32-bit address format, allowing for a total of $2^{32} = 4,294,967,296$ (more than 4.2 billion) addresses. With the global population approaching this number, IPv4 address exhaustion is a foreseeable issue. In contrast, IPv6 employs a 128-bit address format, capable of accommodating an astonishing $2^{128} = 340,282,366,920,938,463,463,463,374,607,$ $431,768$ (more than 340 decillion) addresses, making it virtually inexhaustible. IPv6 also brings various improvements over IPv4. However, the challenge lies in its incompatibility with IPv4, which has hindered its widespread adoption despite its standardization in 1995.

7.5.3 Domain Name

An IP address is made up of digits, which are not easy to remember and use. To make it easier to remember and use, domain names, which are made up of characters, are used. Figure 7.8 shows an illustrative URL, where the portion beginning with "example" represents the domain name. A domain name has a hierarchical structure that is separated by ".". The hierarchy begins with a top-level domain (TLD) situated at the far right, followed by a second-level domain (SLD). The top-level domain can encompass either a generic TLD (gTLD) or a country code TLD (ccTLD). Examples of gTLDs include .com (for companies), .org (for organizations), and .gov (for U.S. government entities).

When a user enters a domain name, such as a website address, the address needs to be converted into its corresponding IP address before it can be used by computers on the Internet. This automatic conversion between domain names and IP addresses is made possible through a mechanism known as the Domain Name System (DNS). DNS servers play a crucial role in managing lists of domain names and their corresponding IP addresses. When a user inputs a domain name, a DNS server translates that name into the corresponding IP address, allowing computers on the Internet to process it. Similarly, when an IP address needs to be converted back into its corresponding domain name, the DNS server handles this translation before presenting the result to the user. Due to the vast number of domain names and IP addresses on the Internet, a single DNS server cannot manage them all effectively. Instead, a

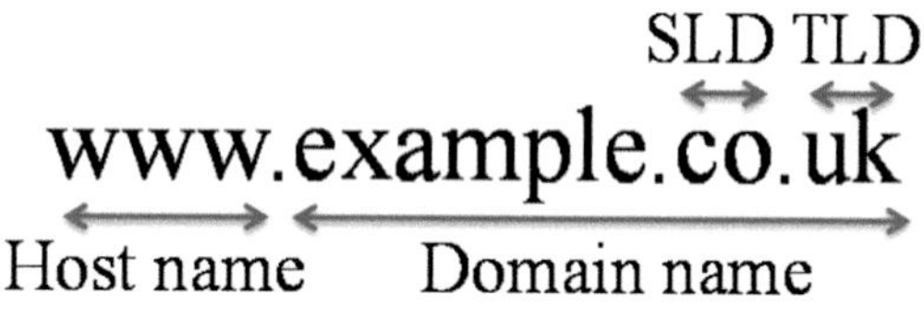

Fig. 7.8 An example of domain name

distributed hierarchical structure is used, with the root DNS server situated at the top.

> • **Questions**
>
> 2. What is the mechanism of a Web page accessible from only inside an institution, i.e. a Web page that cannot be accessed even if you enter your user name and password when you are outside that institution?
>
>   Hint: think about how you can know whether a terminal device is inside the institution.

7.6 Various Information Systems

In recent years, there has been rapid development in information and communication systems, resulting in the popularity of various new systems. In this book, we will provide brief descriptions of some of these systems.

(1) Cloud computing

Cloud computing refers to the use of devices or services over the Internet. The term "cloud" symbolizes the Internet, because Internet is often depicted as a cloud in images.

Traditionally, we have used computers with locally installed software and applications. Cloud computing, however, entails the use of software, applications, and services via the Internet, eliminating the need for installation on local devices. For example, using online services or storing files in online storage are examples of cloud computing.

Cloud computing includes Software as a Service (SaaS), which provides use of software, and Infrastructure as a Service (IaaS), which provides use of computer resources (CPU, memory, storage, etc.) via virtualization technologies.

(2) Sensor network

A sensor network is a type of network in which sensors are interconnected. Originally, the term "network" referred to a system of interconnected computers. In a sensor network, sensors replace the traditional computers. Sensors typically serve specific functions and are simpler than computers. As a result, most sensor networks are wireless and use low-power protocols like ZigBee.

(3) Ubiquitous computing

The word "ubiquitous" derives from the Latin word "ubique", which means "everywhere, anytime, and any place". Accordingly, ubiquitous computing refers to an information environment in which computers are accessible everywhere at any time.

In recent years, the development of smartphones and wearable computers has made it possible for users to own and carry multiple computing devices. As a result, the vision of a ubiquitous networked society based on ubiquitous computing is becoming a reality.

(4) Internet of Things (IoT)

The Internet of things (IoT) is often seen as the successor to ubiquitous computing. IoT has gathered attention because it enables information exchange and control between various things, including home appliances, machines, and portable devices, by assigning them IP addresses directly. IoT facilitates remote control of devices like television recorders and air conditioners, as well as remote monitoring, such as tracking a machine's status or a pet's location. Moreover, it enables seamless communication between things, as they can send and receive data. Furthermore, sensors attached to these things can collect substantial amounts of data, which can open the door to new values and services.

(5) Industry 4.0

Industry 4.0 represents a transformative approach to digitizing and computerizing the manufacturing industry through the integration of AI and IoT. Its primary goal is to enhance productivity by harnessing AI technologies, such as machine learning, for predicting equipment malfunctions and abnormalities. Additionally, it leverages IoT to collect real-time data on machine operations and captures big data like temperature and humidity datasets at various machine locations.

Exercises

1. What may cause a computer network to be slow?

> **• Guidance**
> Think about various possibilities, primarily based on the content in this book.

2. What may cause a computer network to go down?

> **• Guidance**
> Think about various possibilities, primarily based on the content in this book.

3. Describe what you expect in your future life and work from technologies such as AI and IoT.

> **• Guidance**
> Give some detailed examples of your expectations. A poor example might be "use AI to raise work efficiency" because it is unclear how to use AI, raise what kind of efficiency, and in what type of work. It would be better to give more details.

4. Create a flowchart to illustrate your idea for using AI and IoT to realize one of the expectations.

> **• Guidance**
> You are encouraged to create a clear and user-friendly flowchart for an innovative idea. Flowchart is the topic of Chap. 2, and you may review it if you need a refresher. The notes on flowcharting will help you improve the quality of your flowchart.

References

1. Andrew ST, David JW (2010) Computer networks, 5th edn. https://csc-knu.github.io/sys-prog/books/Andrew%20S.%20Tanenbaum%20-%20Computer%20Networks.pdf
2. Forouzan BA (2005) Data communications and networking. McGraw-Hill Education, New Delhi, India
3. https://www.med.kanazawa-u.ac.jp/inside/net/shinsei/listip.html

Chapter 8
Database

8.1 What is a Database

The term "database" can refer to either a collection of data or a database management system.

When referring to a collection of data, it implies a set of items that share common attributes. Examples of such collections include student name lists, customer records, and the vast amounts of data collected by the Internet of Things (IoT). Additionally, the storage media used for housing data, such as magnetic tapes, hard disks, CDs, and USB drives, can also be referred to as databases.

When referring to a database management system, it is a software component for file management in the operating system. In earlier times, such systems were often referred to as "data banks", but today they are commonly known as "databases".

In the early days of computing, a computer capable of handling 100 tasks was priced at $10,000, whereas a new computer capable of handling 1000 tasks was often priced at $50,000; hence, many companies frequently replaced their old computers. However, frequent replacements brought about more problems than just cost-performance ratio. Managers began analyzing the data stored and managed on each computer and discovered significant duplication, leading to poor memory efficiency. As a result, they decided to consolidate the data managed by each computer and created a shared database, marking the start of database management systems [1].

Database management systems will become more important in the future because they play a vital role in supporting decision-making in our daily life and work.

8.2 Relational Database

In routine office work, commands can be used in a database management system called the relational database [2]. Relational databases have several key characteristics, including clarity, data independence, non-procedural data manipulation, and compatibility with distributed databases. Additionally, the efficiency of data reading and writing, which was once considered a drawback, has seen significant improvements.

Table 8.1 illustrates the basic structure of a relational database. In a relational database, a table is often referred to as a "relation", and the relation name is usually positioned in the upper-left corner of the table. Each relation consists of multiple attributes, which are represented as individual columns.

Users can search for attribute values both vertically and horizontally in relational databases as well as perform various operations, similar to commands. Dr. E. F. Codd, the inventor of the relational database, introduced several fundamental operations to the database, and the following are five commonly used ones.

(1) Union
(2) Difference
(3) Intersection
(4) Restriction
(5) Projection

Union, difference, and intersection are applicable to compatible relations, whereas restriction and projection are applicable to a single relation.

Compatible relations are defined by two criteria: (1) The relations must have the same number of attributes, i.e. the same number of columns. (2) They must have the same content for each attribute, regardless of the attribute names. For example, Table 8.2 "IEEE (Institute of Electrical and Electronics Engineers) members" and Table 8.3 "ACIS (Association for Computing and Information Sciences) members" are two compatible relations. They both have three columns, satisfying the first condition. In both relations, the first column contains names, the second column contains age, and the third column contains affiliation, meeting the second condition. Despite having different attribute names in the first row, these relations are compatible.

It should be noted that data in this chapter is fictional with no association with any real-world cases and is used only for illustrative purposes. In the following, we detail union, difference, and intersection, which are applicable to compatible relations.

Table 8.1 Structure of a relation

Relation name

Attribute 1	Attribute 2	...	Attribute m

Table 8.2 IEEE members

Name	Age	Affiliation
John Smith	59	Duke University
Anna Miller	42	IBM
Taro Ito	47	Sony
Yi Zhang	54	Wuhan University

Table 8.3 ACIS members

Designation	Years old	Employed by
Yi Zhang	54	Wuhan University
Mike Taylor	32	University of London
Cihon Lee	49	Samsung

8.2.1   Union

The union operation is commonly used to form the parent set. It creates the set A ∪ B, which is the sum of two sets, A and B, as illustrated in Fig. 8.1.

Table 8.4 shows the result of applying a union operation to the two relations, Tables 8.2 and 8.3. It combines all the rows from both relations, excluding any duplicates.

The resulting relation should be named by combining the names of the two original relations with the " ∪ " symbol. The resulting attribute names should be the same as those of the first relation, in this case, relation A. The data in the result should

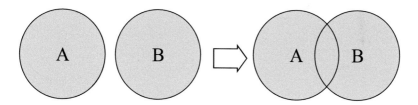

Fig. 8.1 Union of sets A and B

Table 8.4 IEEE members ∪ ACIS members

Name	Age	Affiliation
John Smith	59	Duke University
Anna Miller	42	IBM
Taro Ito	47	Sony
Yi Zhang	54	Wuhan University
Mike Taylor	32	University of London
Cihon Lee	49	Samsung

be a combination of the data from both original relations, representing a member of either IEEE or ACIS.

Redundancy is not allowed in union or other operations applicable to compatible relations. Redundancy occurs when the same data is duplicated within the result. The data "Yi Zhang, 54, Wuhan University" is present in both relations A and B, having it appear twice in the result would cause redundancy. Therefore, the process of ensuring that "Yi Zhang, 54, Wuhan University" appears only once in the result is known as removing redundancy.

8.2.2 Difference

The difference operation is often used as a constraint for data in the parent set. It creates the set A − B, which is the difference between two sets, A and B, as illustrated in Fig. 8.2.

Table 8.5 displays the result of performing a difference operation between Tables 8.2 and 8.3. This operation subtracts the second relation from the first, retaining only the attributes that differ between the two relations.

The resulting relation should be named by connecting the names of the two original relations by a minus symbol "−". The resulting attribute names should be the same as those of the first relation, i.e. relation A. The data in the result should consist of the data from relation A that are not found in relation B, i.e. members of IEEE who are not members of ACIS.

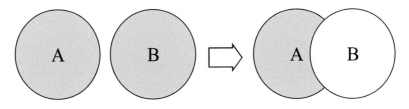

Fig. 8.2 Difference between sets A and B

Table 8.5 IEEE members − ACIS members

Name	Age	Affiliation
John Smith	59	Duke University
Anna Miller	42	IBM
Taro Ito	47	Sony

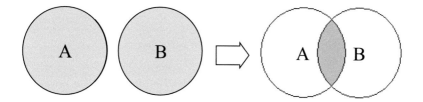

Fig. 8.3 Intersection of sets A and B

Table 8.6 IEEE members ∩
ACIS members

Name	Age	Affiliation
Yi Zhang	54	Wuhan University

8.2.3 Intersection

The intersection operation is often used as a constraint for data within the parent set. It extracts the common elements of two sets, A and B, as illustrated in Fig. 8.3.

Table 8.6 displays the result of applying the intersection operation to the two relations Tables 8.2 and 8.3. This operation extracts the rows that appear in both relations.

The resulting relation should be named by connecting the names of the two original relations by the " ∩ " symbol. The resulting attribute names should be the same as those of the first relation, i.e. relation A. The data in the result should be those that are present in both relation A and relation B, i.e. members who belong to both IEEE and ACIS.

8.2.4 Restriction

The restriction operation retrieves data that satisfy a constraint formula $A_i\theta A_j$. In this formula, A_i and A_j represent attributes, and θ is one of the operators $\{>, <, =, \neq, \geq, \leq\}$. The resulting relation, $R[A_i\theta A_j]$, contains data for which the formula $A_i\theta A_j$ holds.

To perform the restriction operation, relation R must be θ-comparable, which means that any value of attribute A_i can be compared with the value of attribute A_j using the operator θ.

Table 8.8 shows an example of getting the list of products requiring replenishment from the data in Table 8.7. The constraint is "stock $\leq$ safety stock". Here, "stock" refers to the current inventory level, and "safety stock" represents the expected quantity to be sold during the time between placing an order and its delivery.

Typically, safety stock is determined using historical data averages. For example, in the case of the first item, "champagne", the safety stock is 10, because it typically

Table 8.7 Inventory

Code	Name	Stock	Safety stock
P0001	Champagne	8	10
P0002	Red wine	11	10
P0003	Brandy	7	9
P0004	White wine	17	11
P0005	Beer	16	12

Table 8.8 Inventory [stock $\leq$ safety stock]

Code	Name	Stock	Safety stock
P0001	Champagne	8	10
P0003	Brandy	7	9

takes one week from order placement to delivery and during this period, approximately 10 bottles are sold on average. As a result, if the current stock falls below 10, there is a risk of running out of inventory before the next scheduled delivery unless an order is placed immediately. Similarly, the stock level for the third product also falls below its safety stock. Therefore, it is necessary to place immediate orders for both products, as shown in the result.

The resulting relation name should follow the format $R[A_i \theta A_j]$, where R is the original relation name and $[A_i \theta A_j]$ is the constraint. The resulting attribute names should be the same as the original attribute names.

In the restriction operation, attributes can undergo various mathematical operations such as multiplication, division, addition, and subtraction with constants. Furthermore, attributes can be compared to constants as well. For example, if you aim to reduce the risk of stockouts by proactively placing orders, you might consider increasing the safety stock by 3. The resulting restriction operation is given in Table 8.9.

Table 8.9 Inventory [stock $\leq$ safety stock $+$ 3]

Code	Name	Stock	Safety stock
P0001	Champagne	8	10
P0002	Red wine	11	10
P0003	Brandy	7	9

8.2.5 Projection

The projection operation is typically used when dealing with a high number of attributes that cannot fit on a single screen or when there is a need to focus on only a few attributes. It extracts specific columns from a relation. Table 8.10 shows an example of a projection operation on the "name" and "stock" attributes in Table 8.7. The result is a vertical view comprising the two projected columns.

Table 8.10 Inventory

Name	Stock
Champagne	8
Red wine	11
Brandy	7
White wine	17
Beer	16

The resulting relation name should be the same as the original relation name. The resulting attribute names should be the same as those of the projected attributes. The data should be the same as those in the projected columns.

Exercises

1. Using the data provided in Tables 8.11 and 8.12, create a projection on the "name" attribute of the products belonging to the set (alcoholic drinks ∪ soft drinks) with a constraint of [stock ≤ safety stock + 2].

Table 8.11 Alcoholic drinks

Code	Name	Stock	Safety stock
P0001	Champagne	8	10
P0002	Red wine	11	10
P0003	Brandy	7	9
P0004	White wine	17	11
P0005	Beer	16	12

Table 8.12 Soft drinks

Number	Product	Stock	Safety stock
P00010	Orange juice	18	10
P00011	Apple juice	14	12
P00012	Red tea	9	9

> • **Guidance**
>
> Steps to solve this problem.
>
> 1. Create the union of the two given sets "alcoholic drinks" and "soft drinks".
> 2. Apply the restriction operation to the relation created in Step 1, filtering for [stock quantity ≤ safety stock + 2].
> 3. Apply the projection operation to the attribute "name" in the relation obtained in Step 2.
>
> The final result after completing all the three steps is necessary, whereas the intermediate results of Steps 1 and 2 are not required. Please pay attention to the relation name: (1) Ensure that you create the relation name; (2) The name should be the outcome of performing the above three operations.

*2. Using the data provided in Table 8.13, which lists foods recommended for providing weekly nutrition, along with foods eaten this week (Table 8.14) and favorite foods (Table 8.15), perform necessary operations to identify the name(s) of the favorite foods that are recommended weekly but have not been eaten this week. Present the result.

Table 8.13 Weekly recommended foods

Code	Food
1	Apple
2	Tomato
3	Carrot
4	Yogurt
5	Fish

Table 8.14 Foods eaten this week

Number	Item
1	Apple
2	Beef
3	Ice cream
4	Milk
5	Fish

Table 8.15 Favorite foods

Number	Item
1	Apple
2	Peach
3	Beef
4	Yogurt
5	Fish

References

1. R Elmasri, Navathe S B (2015) Fundamentals of database systems, 7th edn. Pearson, Hoboken, NJ. https://amirsmvt.github.io/Database/Static_files/Fundamental_of_Database_Systems.pdf
2. Silberschatz A, Korth HF, Sudarshan S (2010) Database system concepts, 6th edn. McGraw-Hill Science Engineering https://www.octawian.ro/fisiere/situri/asor/build/html/_downloads/1fcab5 3a6d916e39c715fc20a9a9c2a8/Silberschatz_A_databases_6th_ed.pdf

Chapter 9
Information Security

9.1 What is Information Security

The Internet of Things (IoT) has revolutionized connectivity, enabling various devices and systems to connect to the Internet. However, this connectivity also introduces security risks that demand attention. Furthermore, when handling databases or big data containing sensitive or personal information, information security is also a critical concern.

Information security, as defined in JIS Q27000:2014, is the practice of maintaining the confidentiality, integrity, and availability of information. This encompasses preserving characteristics such as authenticity, accountability, non-repudiation, and reliability [1]. For detailed definitions of these terms, please refer to Table 9.1.

Among them, confidentiality, integrity, and availability are called three major elements of information security, as shown in Fig. 9.1. They serve distinct purposes: confidentiality aims to prevent information leakage, integrity safeguards against tampering and data loss, and availability ensures access to necessary data when required. Enhancing confidentiality and integrity can effectively reduce the risk of information leakage and data falsification. However, taking extreme measures to achieve this can result in significantly decreased availability. Conversely, when availability is a top priority, maintaining high levels of confidentiality and integrity might be challenging. These three elements are often in tension with one another, making it crucial to strike a well-balanced approach in considering them.

Table 9.1 Characteristics of information security

Confidentiality	The characteristic of being inaccessible or unusable by unauthorized individuals, entities, and processes
Integrity	The characteristic of safeguarding the authenticity and completeness of information assets
Availability	The characteristic of being accessible and usable by authorized entities upon request
Authenticity	The characteristic of ensuring that an entity or resource matches its claimed identity
Accountability	The characteristic of ensuring that the actions of an entity can be uniquely tracked, either from the action itself or from the entity
Non-repudiation	The characteristic of verifying the undeniable occurrence of an activity or event
Reliability	The characteristic of aligning with intended actions and results

Fig. 9.1 Three major elements of information security

9.2 Risks, Threats, and Vulnerabilities

The primary objective of information security is to safeguard valuable information assets [2]. Information assets include personal information, such as credit card numbers, user IDs, and passwords for individuals, as well as customer information, confidential data, and accounting records for organizations and companies. It is crucial for both individuals and organizations to shield their information assets from potential risks, such as falsification, theft, destruction, and loss. Detailed examples of such risks include theft or loss through removable storage media, network breaches, social engineering attacks, unauthorized access, or the loss of personal computers and smartphones, as illustrated in Fig. 9.2.

A risk arises from threats to the vulnerability of information assets and has the potential to cause damage [2]. The level of risk is determined by the value of information assets, the level of threat, and the degree of vulnerability (Eq. 9.1). Minimizing

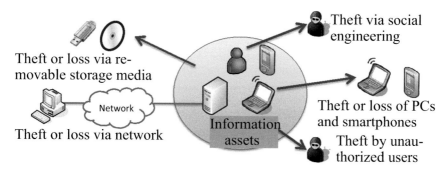

Fig. 9.2 Security risks for information assets

risk is crucial in information security.

$$
\text{Information security risk} = \text{value of information asset} \\
\times \text{level of threat} \times \text{degree of vulnerability} \tag{9.1}
$$

Potential sources of threats and vulnerabilities include human, physical, and technical factors.

(1) **Threats and Vulnerabilities from Human Factors** (Table 9.2)

Potential threats from human factors include those resulting from human errors and social engineering. Social engineering includes various techniques, such as shoulder hacking, i.e. observing someone entering a password by looking over their shoulder, and password spoofing, i.e. identity fraud over the phone to trick individuals into revealing their passwords.

Table 9.2 Threats and vulnerabilities from human factors

Threats	Vulnerabilities
Human error • Maloperation due to assumptions • Unintended operating mistakes	• Illness, fatigue, excessive workload • Misunderstanding or inadequate understanding of operations • Misleading information in operating manuals
Sabotage • Laziness or inattention to security rules	• Inadequate operator management • Inadequate education about obeying rules • Inadequate punishment for breaking rules
Internal crime • Intentional theft of information by personnel within the organization	• Inadequate operator management • Inadequate access management • Inadequate punishment for breaking rules
Social engineering • Theft of passwords • Theft of information by impersonating an administrator	• Inadequate knowledge about social engineering techniques

(2) **Threats and Vulnerabilities from Physical Factors** (Table 9.3)

Environmental physical threats include various sources, such as natural disasters, equipment failures, and physical destruction. Vulnerabilities often stem from inadequate equipment and facility management. Effective countermeasures, such as equipment redundancy, can reduce these physical threats.

(3) **Threats and Vulnerabilities from Technical Factors** (Table 9.4)

Threats resulting from technical factors often involve intentional actions. Technical threats include a range of issues, such as unauthorized access, eavesdropping, Denial-of-Service (DoS) attacks, and computer viruses. These actions fall under the category of cybercrimes. A common technical vulnerability is a "security hole", which refers to a bug or defect in the operating system or software that may lead to technical threats. Therefore, when a security hole is identified, it is essential to fix it promptly to maintain security.

Table 9.3 Threats and vulnerabilities from physical factors

Threats	Vulnerabilities
Natural disasters • Fire, earthquake • Thunderstorm (including blackout caused by lightning)	• Lack of fireproofing and earthquake-proofing measures • Inadequate lightning strike surge protection
Equipment failure • Equipment failure or loss not caused by natural disasters	• Inadequate equipment failure measures (redundancy and updates) • Incorrect equipment setting • Inadequate equipment rental management
Intruders • Physical damage by intruders • Theft of equipment by intruders	• Inadequate lock management for equipment areas • Inadequate entrance/exit management for equipment areas

Table 9.4 Threats and vulnerabilities from technical factors

Threats	Vulnerabilities
Unauthorized access • Impersonation, cracking	• Security holes in information devices and software
Eavesdropping • Phishing scams, spyware	• Inadequate anti-virus measures • Inadequate education about attack techniques • Security holes in information devices and software
DoS attacks • Denial-of-Service (DoS) attacks, distributed DoS (DDoS) attacks	• Inadequate measures against DoS attacks • Security holes in information devices and software
Computer viruses • Malware • Worms, Trojans, bots	• Inadequate anti-virus measures • Inadequate education about attack techniques • Security holes in information devices and software

• **Questions**

1. How can you prevent the leakage of recipients' personal information (email addresses) when sending an email to multiple recipients who do not know each other?

   Hint: think about where to enter recipients' email addresses, such as in the new message window of Outlook (Fig. 9.3).

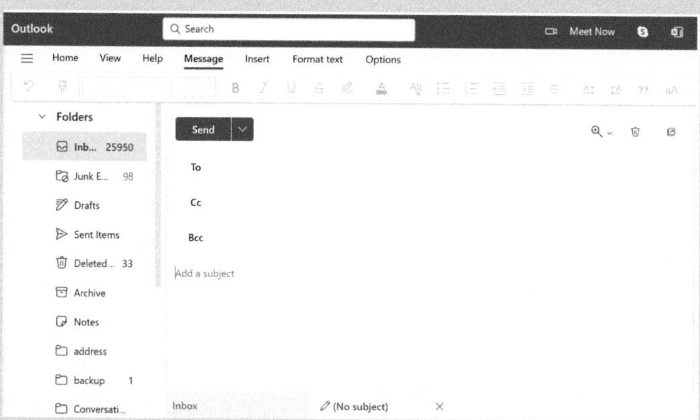

Fig. 9.3 New message window in Outlook

   Please note that not all questions in this chapter can be answered based on the content of this book. For questions without answers in the book, feel free to respond based on your experience or personal understanding.

2. Choose the incorrect items for managing a USB disk containing personal information (multiple choices allowed).

   A. Leaving it in a bag in your car before locking the car and going to eat at a restaurant.
   B. Leaving it on the desk in your university lab before locking the lab door and going home.
   C. Taking it with you when going home.

9.3   Security Measures for Users

9.3.1   Management of User IDs and Passwords

A combination of a user ID (account) and password is commonly used for user authentication in determining access to an information system. A user ID is a system-registered identifier designed to uniquely identify a user, whereas a password is a string of characters known only to the user. Effective password management practices include: (1) Not sharing your password with others. (2) Using unique passwords for different systems. (3) Avoiding writing down the combination of user ID and password on paper. (4) Not using easily guessable passwords, such as birthdays or dictionary words.

> • **Questions**
>
> 3.   Do you think setting a login password ensures computer security? Why?

9.3.2   Anti-virus Measures

Malware and computer viruses, in a broad sense, refer to programs designed to intentionally harm software or data. In a narrower sense, they are defined as programs that are:

- Self-replicate: capable of infecting other programs or systems by copying themselves.
- Latent: can remain hidden, with symptoms appearing only under specific conditions, like at a specified time, after a set amount of time, or after a certain number of executions.
- Pathogenic: can destroy files, such as programs and data, and operate in ways unintended by the user.

While viruses can exploit system vulnerabilities, they are frequently introduced into a system through files downloaded from the Internet or email attachments. A vital measure for protection is to use anti-virus software to scan external files for viruses. Nevertheless, installing anti-virus software alone is insufficient. Regularly update your anti-virus software with the latest virus definition files. Additionally, it is recommended to keep the operating system, software, and applications up to date while addressing any security vulnerabilities within them.

Table 9.5 Access rights and settings

Access rights	Read	Rights to read files and folders
	Write	Rights to create and overwrite files and folders
	Modify	Rights to read, write, and delete files and folders
	Full control	Rights to fully access files and folders, and modify access rights settings
Settings	Enable	Enable access
	Disable	Disable access (takes priority over the enable option)
	Empty	Inherit the settings of the parent folder

9.4 Security Measures for Administrators

9.4.1 Create Information Security Policy

One important security measure is the creation of information security policy, establishing fundamental principles for ensuring information security. Information security policy is particularly effective in addressing threats from humans. This policy helps define the rules for handling information assets and establishes a system for compliance with these rules.

9.4.2 Access Management

System administrators should implement security measures to control and restrict access to information assets. These measures may include a combination of physical and electronic security measures. Physical security measures can regulate access to facilities where information assets are stored through the use of physical keys, integrated circuit (IC) cards, and biometric authentication. Electronic security measures can manage access to data, including files and folders, by defining access rights for individual users or groups. Access rights can be customized for each specific file and folder. Table 9.5 presents an overview of the available access rights and settings.

9.4.3 Firewall

Another security measure is the use of a firewall. A firewall is a communication device employed to safeguard client PCs in an internal network against potential threats from the Internet. The firewall functions by scrutinizing packets that traverse the connection point between the internal network and the Internet. It determines whether to permit or block the transmission of incoming packets based on their IP addresses and the applications using them. Its fundamental operation allows requests from clients in the internal network whereas rejecting requests from the Internet, with exceptions made as needed (as shown in Fig. 9.4).

For communication initiated by a client on the internal network, a mechanism called stateful packet inspection (SPI) is used to maintain the communication status and allow replies from the Internet to pass through temporarily (Fig. 9.5).

When a server is accessible to the public Internet, it is a common security practice to isolate its network environment from the rest of the organization's devices due to external threats. This isolated area between the Internet and the internal network is known as a Demilitarized Zone (DMZ). The relation between a firewall and a DMZ is illustrated in Fig. 9.6. Using a firewall to regulate communication between the Internet and the DMZ enhances security, reducing threats from the Internet and enabling secure use of Internet services from the internal network.

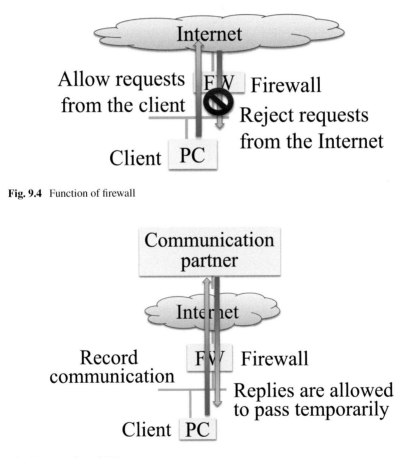

Fig. 9.4 Function of firewall

Fig. 9.5 Function of SPI

Fig. 9.6 Function of DMZ

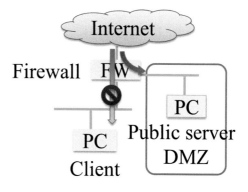

9.5 Security Technologies

Encryption and authentication are security technologies that help maintain confidentiality and integrity. In the following, we will provide detailed explanations of these two technologies.

9.5.1 Encryption

Encryption is a technology that makes digital data unreadable to unauthorized parties. It involves the transformation of plain text into ciphertext, a form of text rendered unreadable through the use of specific keys or rules. The reverse process, turning ciphertext back into plain text, is known as decryption. Encryption serves two primary purposes: it safeguards data and communication paths to prevent eavesdropping, ensuring confidentiality, and it guarantees the integrity of transmitted data by preventing tampering during transit.

There are two main types of encryption systems: symmetric key cryptosystem and public key cryptosystem [2].

The symmetric key cryptosystem, in use for a long time, employs the same key for both encryption and decryption. While it requires the sender and receiver to share the key beforehand, it offers the advantage of being simple and both encryption and decryption processes are fast (Fig. 9.7). Data Encryption Standard (DES), Triple DES (3DES), and Advanced Encryption Standard (AES) are three standards for encryption. DES has a key length of only 56 bits, and hence is no longer recommended due to low encryption strength. AES is currently the mainstream standard.

In the public key cryptosystem, the keys used for encryption and decryption are separate, as depicted in Fig. 9.8. This system requires two types of keys: a public key and a private key, which are used in pairs. The public key is accessible to anyone, whereas the private key is available to only the key owner. The system operates either using the public key for encryption and its paired private key for decryption or using the private key for encryption and its paired public key for decryption. If data

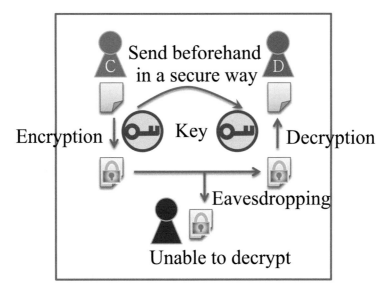

Fig. 9.7 Symmetric key cryptosystem

is encrypted with the public key, it can only be decrypted using the corresponding private key, and vice versa.

When the public key is used for encryption and the private key is used for decryption, there is no need to transmit the decryption key through the communication

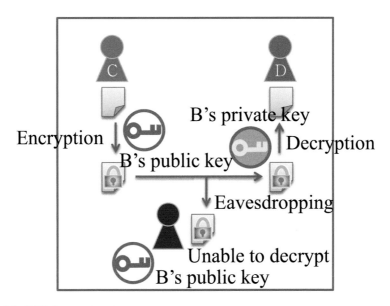

Fig. 9.8 Public key cryptosystem

channel. Therefore, the challenge of sharing keys before communication is eliminated. If the private key is used for encryption and the public key is used for decryption, it allows for data creator authentication. However, it is important to note that the public key cryptosystem is more complex than the symmetric key cryptosystem, and the encryption and decryption processes tend to be slower. The encryption method typically employs the Rivest, Shamir, Adleman (RSA) algorithm, known for its difficulty in factoring the product of two prime numbers.

9.5.2 Digital Signature and Digital Authentication

While encryption effectively safeguards against threats like eavesdropping and data falsification, it faces challenges when it comes to preventing user spoofing. To address this problem, a mechanism known as digital signature is employed. A digital signature uses the public key cryptosystem to encrypt a message using the user's private key. The user's identity will be confirmed if the encrypted message can be decrypted using the corresponding public key.

To verify a user's identity using a digital signature, it is crucial to confirm the rightness of their public key. This verification process is facilitated by the Public Key Infrastructure (PKI), a global authentication system. PKI employs digital certificates to validate the public key's authenticity and the user's trustworthiness. Digital certificates are issued and managed by certificate authorities. Users are required to preregister their public keys with a trusted certificate authority, which then issues a digital certificate. This combination of a digital signature and a digital certificate, like a real-world seal and a seal certificate, enables digital authentication and is often referred to as e-authentication.

9.5.3 Secure Encrypted Communication

Secure Socket Layer (SSL) was initially a protocol for encrypted communication using public key authentication. Subsequently, it was standardized under the name Transport Layer Security (TLS), though SSL remains a more common term.

SSL-based encrypted communication combines the advantages of both symmetric key cryptography and public key cryptography. It achieves this by encrypting communication data using a symmetric key, which, in turn, is encrypted with a public key. Using a symmetric key for data encryption reduces the processing load for both encryption and decryption, enhancing efficiency. Encrypting the symmetric key using a public key increases security. The public key of the communication partner, such as a web server, can be obtained from a digital certificate through public key authentication.

SSL operates at the transport/application layer in the TCP/IP model and can be used in many applications. One of its primary and widespread uses is in the form

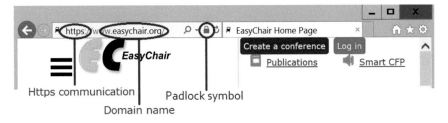

Fig. 9.9 Website using HTTPS

of HTTP Secure (HTTPS), which ensures encrypted communication on the World Wide Web (WWW).

A URL using HTTPS begins with "https://". When the digital signature of the target server is successfully verified, a padlock symbol appears in the URL bar, and the background color may turn green. These indicators signal to the user that the website is secure. For example, Fig. 9.9 shows the URL of a website using HTTPS.

Exercises

1. According to the content of this book, is it possible to use artificial intelligence (AI) to detect a virus? if so, please briefly explain the mechanism.
*2. Describe the conflicting nature of the three major elements of information security.
*3. Describe the difference between the symmetric key cryptosystem and public key cryptosystem.

References

1. Information technology—security technology—information security management systems—terminology (JIS Q27000: 2014), Japanese Industrial Standards
2. Whitman ME, Mattord HJ (2012) Principles of information security, 4th ed. Cengage Learning, Boston, MA. http://almuhammadi.com/sultan/sec_books/Whitman.pdf

Chapter 10
Solutions to Exercises

10.1 Chapter 1 Solutions and Answers

Answers to Questions:

1. A smartphone is a programmable electronic digital computing device, and hence, it can be considered a computer. The programs running on a smartphone are commonly referred to as applications or "apps".

Solutions to Exercises:

1. See Table 10.1.

Table 10.1 Truth table of multiplying two bits

Input		Output
A	B	P
0	0	0
0	1	0
1	0	0
1	1	1

$$P = A \times B$$

It is not mandatory to name the input and output variables as A, B, and P, but P is a suitable choice to represent "product", which aligns with multiplication. You have the flexibility to use other letters for variable names. There is no need to include Column C.

2. See Table 10.2.

Table 10.2 Truth table of the circuit in Fig. 1.14

Input				Output
A	B	a	b	X
0	0	1	0	0
0	1	1	1	1
1	0	0	1	0
1	1	0	1	0

➡

Input		Output
A	B	X
0	0	0
0	1	1
1	0	0
1	1	0

Table 10.3 Truth table of A AND B AND C

Input			Output
A	B	C	X
0	0	0	0
0	0	1	0
0	1	0	0
0	1	1	0
1	0	0	0
1	0	1	0
1	1	0	0
1	1	1	1

Since "a" and "b" serve as intermediate variables in obtaining the final result, it is better to exclude them from the final result.

*3. See Table 10.3.
*4. See Table 10.4.
*5. See Fig 10.1.

Table 10.4 Truth table of NOT (A AND (B OR C))

Input			Output
A	B	C	X
0	0	0	1
0	0	1	1
0	1	0	1
0	1	1	1
1	0	0	1
1	0	1	0
1	1	0	0
1	1	1	0

Fig. 10.1 Circuit for NOT
(A AND (B OR C))

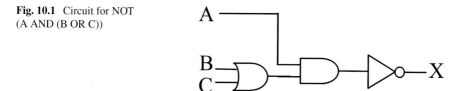

10.2 Chapter 2 Solutions and Answers

1. See Fig. 10.2.

Points

1. Initialize both the counter and the timer/alarm.
2. Create the steps "jump up once" and "$j = j + 1$" as a paired set of instructions. Including the increase of "j" is necessary because counting is a required action.
3. Avoid including a step such as "timer = timer + 1" since the duration of each jump may not be exactly one time unit, and there is no need to advance time.

Fig. 10.2 Flowchart of the jumping exercise

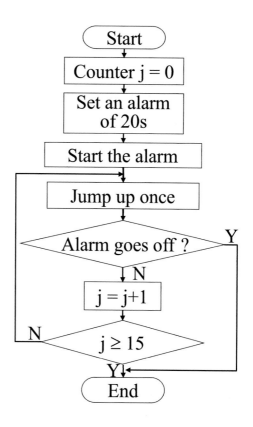

10.3   Chapter 3 Solutions and Answers

1. $O(n^3)$

In the polynomial $8n^3 + 10000n + 83417$, the term with the biggest effect is $8n^3$. Replacing the coefficient 8 with 1 yields n^3, and placing n^3 inside the ( ) after the big O results in the time complexity.

2. $O(n^2)$

Figure 10.3 shows the range of E, where the highlighted part when n is very large, should be focused on. In this part, the upper bound is $2n^2 - 100$. Time complexity represents the time required for the largest possible value of n, and hence the upper bound determines the time complexity. In the upper bound polynomial, $2n^2$ is the term with the biggest effect. Replacing the coefficient 2 with 1 yields n^2, and placing n^2 in the ( ) after the big O results in the time complexity.

3. $O(1)$

The number of iterations R of the loop is 10. If the number of iterations is a constant, the time complexity will be $O(1)$.

*4. $O(n\log n)$

Similar to exercise problem 2, replace the coefficient 3 in "3lognn" with 1, and express the result "lognn" in a more comprehensible form as "$n\log n$". Place this in the parentheses following the big O. Note that "log" without a specified base implies that the base can be any number.

*5. $O(n)$

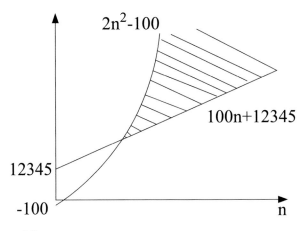

Fig. 10.3 Range of E

The number of iterations of the loops is 100n. Specifically, the number of iterations of the loop right below "$i = 100$" is 100, and of the loop right below "$j = n$" is n. In total, the number of iterations is $100 \times n = 100n$. The total number of instructions is $(3n + 3) \times 100 + 1 = 300n + 301$. In either case, replacing the coefficient before "n" with 1 yields "n", resulting in a time complexity of $O(n)$. In other words, time complexity can be obtained from either the total number of instructions or the number of iterations of the most iterated loop.

10.4   Chapter 4 Solutions and Answers

Answers to Questions

1. $n!$

The number of jobs that can be processed the first is "n". After processing the first job, the number of jobs that can be processed the second is "$n - 1$". Similarly, the number of jobs that can be processed the third is "$n - 2$". In other words, after each job is processed, the number of remaining jobs decreases by one. This leads to a total number of processing sequences to be $n \times (n - 1) \times (n - 2) \times \ldots \times 1 = n!$

2. $O(n!)$

The iteration for calculating the objective function value in the exhaustive search is shown in Fig. 10.4. Since the number of iterations R of the loop is $n!$, the time complexity is $O(n!)$.

3. Second
4. Job 2
5. Yes
6. $n!$
7. $O(n!)$

The number of cities that can be visited the first is "n". After visiting the first city, the number of cities that can be visited the second is "$n - 1$". Similarly, the number

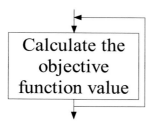

Number of iterations = number of processing sequences = n!

Fig. 10.4 Number of iterations

of cities that can be visited the third is "$n - 2$". In other words, after each city is visited, the number of remaining cities decreases by one. This leads to a total number of visiting sequences to be $n \times (n - 1) \times (n - 2) \times \ldots \times 1 = n!$

Solutions to Exercises

1.

Notation

c index of city$(c = 1, 2, \ldots, n)$

i order of visit$(i = 1, 2, \ldots, n)$

C_i ith city to visit

$d_{Ci, Ci+1}$ distance between C_i and C_{i+1}

Objective function: Minimize $\sum_{i=1}^{n-1} d_{C_i, C_{i+1}}$

It is important to define order of visit. Alternatively, you can define only "ith city to visit" or "distance between the ith and the $(i + 1)$th cities to visit". In the objective function, the iteration of "i" concludes at "$n - 1$" rather than "n" because the last distance is from the $i = (n - 1)$th city to the $i + 1 = n$th city.

If the salesman needs to return to the initial city after visiting the nth city, the iteration of "i" can conclude at "n". In this textbook, we assume that it is allowed for the starting point to be different from the finishing point. Hence, the mission is considered finished when the salesman completes the visit to the nth city.

To enhance your understanding and problem-solving ability, some common incorrect solutions are listed below.

Incorrect solution 1:

c index of city$(c = 1, 2, \ldots, n)$

$d_{c, c+1}$ distance between c and $c + 1$

Objective function: Minimize $\sum_{c=1}^{n-1} d_{c, c+1}$

If c represents index of city, then $d_{1, 2}$ represents the distance between city 1 and city 2, and $d_{2, 3}$ represents the distance between city 2 and city 3. Accordingly, the objective function expresses only one visiting sequence: city 1 $\rightarrow$ city 2 $\rightarrow$ city 3 $\rightarrow$ city 4 $\rightarrow$ city 5. It cannot express other sequences such as city 2 $\rightarrow$ city 5 $\rightarrow$ city 3 $\rightarrow$ city 1 $\rightarrow$ city 4.

Incorrect solution 2:

i, j index of city$(i = 1, 2, \ldots, n \quad j = 1, 2, \ldots, n)$

$d_{i, j}$ distance between city i and city j

Objective function: Minimize $\sum_{i=1}^{i=n} \sum_{j=1}^{j=n} d_{i,j}, i \neq j$

Let us use three cities as an example with i and j both ranging from 1 to 3. Initially, with $i = 1$ and $j = 2$ and 3, $\sum_j d_{i, j}$ calculates the distance between city 1 and city 2 (distance 1) + the distance between city 1 and city 3 (distance 2). Then, with $i = 2$ and $j = 1$ and 3, $\sum_j d_{i,j}$ calculates the distance between city 2 and city 1 (distance 3) + the distance between city 2 and city 3 (distance 4). Finally, with $i = 3$ and $j = 1$ and 2, $\sum_j d_{i,j}$ calculates the distance between city 3 and city 1 (distance 5) + the distance between city 3 and city 2 (distance 6). In total, $\sum_i \sum_j d_{i,j}$ sums up distances 1 to 6, which amounts to twice the total distance between all cities, rather than the distance of visiting three cities at a time.

Incorrect solution 3:

i, j index of city$(i = 1, 2, \ldots, n \quad j = 1, 2, \ldots, n)$
$d_{i,j}$ distance between city i and city j
$X_{i,j}$ $X_{i,j} = 1$ means the route is taken
$\phantom{X_{i,j}}$ $X_{i,j} = 0$ means the route is not taken

Objective function: Minimize $\sum_{i=1}^{i=n} \sum_{j=1}^{j=n} d_{i,j} \times X_{i,j}, i \neq j$

This model needs constraints to ensure that the solution is feasible. Without constraints, it is possible that the end of one route is not connected to the start of the next route, as depicted in Fig. 10.5. In Fig. 10.5a, the number of routes taken is insufficient to visit all the cities, and the routes are not connected. In Fig. 10.5b, the number of routes taken is correct, and the routes are connected but not in a way that allows the trip to be completed in one go. Therefore, this model is only correct when constraints are added to prevent such infeasible solutions. However, the constraints can be complex, particularly for beginners, so we will not delve into the details here.

2. An example of encoding:

i 1 2 3 $\ldots$ n

C_i | 2 n 1 $\ldots$ 3 |

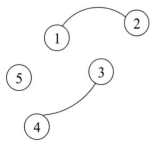 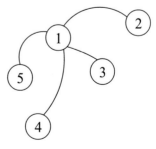

(a) Two routes whose $X_{i,j} = 1$ (b) Four routes whose $X_{i,j} = 1$

Fig. 10.5 Examples of infeasible solutions

*3.   Another way of encoding:

$$c \quad 1 \ 2 \ 3 \ \dots \ n$$

$$i \quad \boxed{3 \ 1 \ n \ \dots \ 2}$$

The first way of encoding means that the first city to visit is city 2, the second city to visit is city n, and the third city to visit is city 1. The second way of encoding means that city 1 is the third city to visit, city 2 is the first city to visit, and city 3 is the nth city to visit.

10.5   Chapter 5 Solutions and Answers

1. Initial population creation and evaluation:

    A   1 2 3 4 5   25+15+20+45=105
    B   2 3 1 5 4   20+5+25+45=95
    C   3 4 5 2 1   15+5+30+40+45=135
    D   4 1 5 2 3   10+5+20+30+45=110
    E   5 3 1 4 2   5+10+15+35+45=110

Selection:

   Elite selection: B (underlined individuals will be in the next generation)
   Tournament selection (k=3): A, C, E → A

Crossover:

   Randomly pick up A and B, suppose r_1=0.7 → crossover
   A   1 2|3 4 5 → 1 2 3 5 4 (Individual F)
   B   2 3|1 5 4 → 2 3 1 4 5 (Individual G)

   Attention: in the produced offspring, the genes inherited from parent A and parent B must maintain the same order as in the parents. In other words, the order of genes 3 5 4 in F and 1 4 5 in G should not be altered.

Mutation:

   Randomly pick up D, suppose r_2=0.1 → mutate
   D   4 1 5 2 3 → 2 1 5 4 3 (Individual H)
Second generation: B · A · F · G · H

Second generation evaluation:

    A   2 3 1 5 4   20+5+25+45=95
    B   1 2 3 4 5   25+15+20+45=105
    C   1 2 3 5 4   25+15+25+45=110
    D   2 3 1 4 5   20+5+20+45=90
    E   2 1 5 4 3   20+15+10+30+45=120

The best found individual B is updated by G, so repeat the reproduction process.

Selection:

Elite selection: G

Tournament selection: A, F, H → A

Crossover:

Randomly pick up B and H, suppose $r_1=0.5$ → crossover

B   2 3|1 5 4 → 2 3 1 5 4 (Individual B)

H   2 1|5 4 3 → 2 1 3 5 4 (Individual I)

Mutation:

Randomly pick up A, suppose $r_2 = 0.3$ → no mutation

Third generation: G · A · B · I · A

Third generation evaluation:

G: 90
A: 105
B: 95
I: 105
A: 105

The best individual G remains the same as in the second generation, so the termination criterion "best found individual is not updated for one generation" is met, and the process is concluded.

Finally, output the objective function value of the best found individual G: 90.

10.6   Chapter 6 Solutions and Answers

Answers to Questions

1. Yes. Set the values of w and θ so that both $0 \geq \theta$ and $w \geq \theta$ are satisfied. For example, $w=2, \theta=-2$.
2. Yes. Set the values of w and θ so that both $0 \geq \theta$ and $w < \theta$ are satisfied. For example, $w = -5, \theta = -4$.
3. A

In TLU learning, the weights and threshold will be updated until the actual output matches the correct output, making it a form of supervised learning.

Solutions to Exercises

1. First, create the truth table of X_1 AND X_2 AND X_3 (Table 10.5).

Table 10.5 Truth table of X_1 AND X_2 AND X_3

Input			Output
X_1	X_2	X_3	T
0	0	0	0
0	0	1	0
0	1	0	0
0	1	1	0
1	0	0	0
1	0	1	0
1	1	0	0
1	1	1	1

Next, create the constraints based on the truth table:

$$w_1 \times 0 + w_2 \times 0 + w_3 \times 0 < \theta \tag{10.1}$$

$$w_1 \times 0 + w_2 \times 0 + w_3 \times 1 < \theta \tag{10.2}$$

$$w_1 \times 0 + w_2 \times 1 + w_3 \times 0 < \theta \tag{10.3}$$

$$w_1 \times 0 + w_2 \times 1 + w_3 \times 1 < \theta \tag{10.4}$$

$$w_1 \times 1 + w_2 \times 0 + w_3 \times 0 < \theta \tag{10.5}$$

$$w_1 \times 1 + w_2 \times 0 + w_3 \times 1 < \theta \tag{10.6}$$

$$w_1 \times 1 + w_2 \times 1 + w_3 \times 0 < \theta \tag{10.7}$$

$$w_1 \times 1 + w_2 \times 1 + w_3 \times 1 \geq \theta \tag{10.8}$$

Calculate Eqs. 10.1–10.8 and get the results:

$$0 < \theta \tag{10.9}$$

$$w_3 < \theta \tag{10.10}$$

$$w_2 < \theta \tag{10.11}$$

Table 10.6 Truth table of the circuit in Fig. 6.15

Input		Output
A	B	T
0	0	1
0	1	1
1	0	0
1	1	1

$$w_2 + w_3 < \theta \tag{10.12}$$

$$w_1 < \theta \tag{10.13}$$

$$w_1 + w_3 < \theta \tag{10.14}$$

$$w_1 + w_2 < \theta \tag{10.15}$$

$$w_1 + w_2 + w_3 \geq \theta \tag{10.16}$$

Finally, set the values of w and θ so that all the constraints are satisfied. For example, $w_1 = 4$, $w_2 = 2$, $w_3 = 2$, $\theta = 7$; $w_1 = 3$, $w_2 = 3$, $w_3 = 3$, $\theta = 9$.

2. First, create the truth table of the given circuit (Table 10.6).

Next, create the constraints based on the truth table:

$$w_1 \times 0 + w_2 \times 0 \geq \theta \tag{10.17}$$

$$w_1 \times 0 + w_2 \times 1 \geq \theta \tag{10.18}$$

$$w_1 \times 1 + w_2 \times 0 < \theta \tag{10.19}$$

$$w_1 \times 1 + w_2 \times 1 \geq \theta \tag{10.20}$$

Calculate Eqs. 10.17–10.20 and get the results:

$$0 \geq \theta \tag{10.21}$$

$$w_2 \geq \theta \tag{10.22}$$

$$w_1 < \theta \tag{10.23}$$

Fig. 10.6 Relation between
AI, ML, and NN

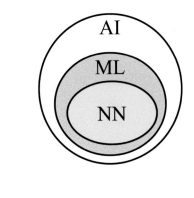

$$w_1 + w_2 \geq \theta \qquad\qquad (10.24)$$

Finally, set the values of w and θ so that all the constraints are satisfied. For example, $w_1 = -4$, $w_2 = 2$, $\theta = -2$; $w_1 = -5$, $w_2 = 5$, $\theta = -4$.

3. See Fig. 10.6.

AI has been our topic since Chap. 4. In Chap. 5, we introduced genetic algorithm, and in Chap. 6, neural network. Neural network is a subset of machine learning, and machine learning is a subset of AI.

*4. See Table 10.7.

Constraints:

$$0 < \theta \qquad\qquad (10.25)$$

$$w_3 < \theta \qquad\qquad (10.26)$$

Table 10.7 Truth table of X_1 AND (X_2 OR X_3)

Input			Output
X_1	X_2	X_3	T
0	0	0	0
0	0	1	0
0	1	0	0
0	1	1	0
1	0	0	0
1	0	1	1
1	1	0	1
1	1	1	1

$$w_2 < \theta \qquad\qquad (10.27)$$

$$w_2 + w_3 < \theta \qquad\qquad (10.28)$$

$$w_1 < \theta \qquad\qquad (10.29)$$

$$w_1 + w_3 \geq \theta \qquad\qquad (10.30)$$

$$w_1 + w_2 \geq \theta \qquad\qquad (10.31)$$

$$w_1 + w_2 + w_3 \geq \theta \qquad\qquad (10.32)$$

An example of w and θ values that satisfy all the constraints: $w_1 = 8, w_2 = 2, w_3 = 2, \theta = 10$.

*5. Create the constraints based on the truth table:

$$0 < \theta \qquad\qquad (10.33)$$

$$w_3 \geq \theta \qquad\qquad (10.34)$$

$$w_2 \geq \theta \qquad\qquad (10.35)$$

$$w_2 + w_3 \geq \theta \qquad\qquad (10.36)$$

$$w_1 \geq \theta \qquad\qquad (10.37)$$

$$w_1 + w_3 \geq \theta \qquad\qquad (10.38)$$

$$w_1 + w_2 \geq \theta \qquad\qquad (10.39)$$

$$w_1 + w_2 + w_3 < \theta \qquad\qquad (10.40)$$

You will notice that there are no values of w and θ that can satisfy all the constraints, and that is why a single TLU cannot produce the same output.

10.7   Chapter 7 Solutions and Answers

Answers to Questions:

1. Frequency band

Wi-Fi operates in two frequency bands: 2.4 and 5 GHz, each with its own merit and demerit.

2.4 GHz:

> Merit: strong ability to go through obstacles
> Demerit: can be interfered by home appliances like microwave ovens because they use the same frequency band

5 GHz:

> Merit: minimal interference because 5 GHz is an exclusive frequency band reserved for Wi-Fi
> Demerit: limited ability to go through obstacles

2. IP address

The range of IP addresses assigned to an institution is pre-established and constant, enabling us to identify whether a terminal is within the institution based on its IP address.

Solutions to Exercises

1.

* Maximum data rate is slow (e.g. 10 Mbps)
* Far from the exchange station in a copper cabling network
* Network is busy due to many accesses
* Obstacles and interference in a Wi-Fi network
* Connection issue, virus infection, data rate restriction, etc.

2.

* Connection issue due to scratches, bends, or stains in a fiber optic cabling network
* Breakdown of a device connecting other devices on the network
* Obstacles or lack of signals in a Wi-Fi network, etc.

3. Some solutions from learners: (1) clothes drying poles that move in automatically when it rains or gets dark, (2) doors that open automatically when the owner returns, (3) car systems that automatically maintain a minimum following distance.

4. Figures 10.7, 10.8 and 10.9 are flowcharts created by some learners for their solutions to problem 3.

Fig. 10.7 Flowchart of an automatic clothes drying pole

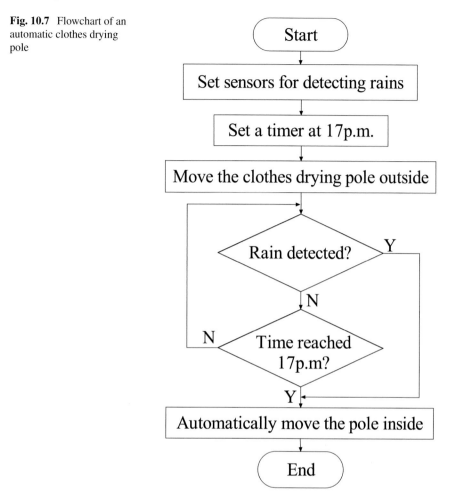

Regarding Fig. 10.9, some explanations are given as follows. According to Japanese driving textbooks, the recommended minimum following distance is (speed − 15) km/h when the vehicle's speed is in the range of 30–70 km/h. If the vehicle's speed exceeds 70 km/h, the minimum following distance should be no less than the vehicle's speed km/h. Figure 10.9 illustrates the control flowchart for achieving this.

10.8   Chapter 8 Solutions and Answers

Solutions to Exercises

1. Step 1: create the union "alcoholic drinks ∪ soft drinks".

Fig. 10.8 Flowchart of an automatic door with face recognition

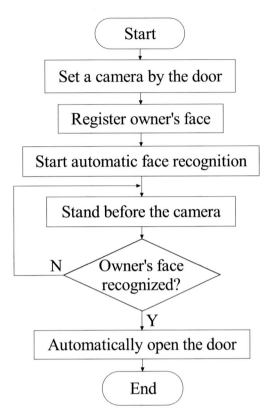

Step 2: apply the restriction "stock ≤ safety stock + 2" to Table 10.8. First calculate "safety stock + 2", with the results displayed on the right side of Table 10.8. Items that meet the condition "stock ≤ safety stock + 2" are shown in bold and underlined. The result of step 2 is presented in Table 10.9.

Step 3: apply the projection on "name" to Table 10.9, and the final result is displayed in Table 10.10. It should be noted that the relation name (table name) remains unchanged when applying projection.

*2.   See Table 10.11.

10.9   Chapter 9 Solutions and Answers

Answers to Questions

1.   Write the recipients' email addresses after "Bcc" rather than "To" or "CC".

It is highly recommended to use the "Bcc" field when sending emails to a group of recipients who may not know each other or should not have access to each other's

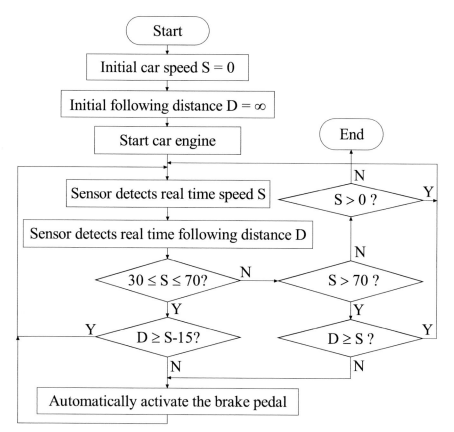

Fig. 10.9 Flowchart of a following distance keeping system

Table 10.8   Alcoholic drinks ∪ soft drinks

Code	Name	Stock	Safety stock	
P0001	Champagne	8	10	**12**
P0002	Red wine	11	10	**12**
P0003	Brandy	7	9	**11**
P0004	White wine	17	11	13
P0005	Beer	16	12	14
P00010	Orange juice	18	10	12
P00011	Apple juice	14	12	**14**
P00012	Red tea	9	9	**11**

Table 10.9 Alcoholic drinks ∪ soft drinks [stock ≤ safety stock + 2]

Code	Name	Stock	Safety stock
P0001	Champagne	8	10
P0002	Red wine	11	10
P0003	Brandy	7	9
P00011	Apple juice	14	12
P00012	Red tea	9	9

Table 10.10 Alcoholic drinks ∪ soft drinks [stock ≤ safety stock + 2]

Name
Champagne
Red wine
Brandy
Apple juice
Red tea

Table 10.11 (Weekly recommended foods − foods eaten this week) ∩ favorite foods

Food
Yogurt

email addresses. With "Bcc", each recipient gets the email without seeing the email addresses of other Bcc recipients. On the other hand, "CC" is used when you want to keep all the recipients informed and be aware of the communication. When you add recipients to the CC field, all the recipients can see the email addresses of everyone else who received the email.

2. A and B

Even when stored in a locked car, a USB drive containing sensitive data is not secure due to the risk of theft and exposure to extreme temperatures. Thieves can gain access to locked cars using lock-picking tools, and extreme temperatures in a car may potentially damage the drive.

Leaving the drive in a lab that is accessible to multiple individuals also poses security risks. Comparing with leaving it in an unattended or potentially vulnerable location, carrying it with you can be more secure due to direct physical control, reduced exposure, and immediate access. Just be cautious not to lose it.

3. Setting a login password alone does not provide a high level of security, because cracking software tools available for download on the Internet can potentially break the login password relatively quickly. Measures such as setting a BIOS password or using hard disk encryption will enhance the level of security.

Solutions to Exercises

1. Before Sect. 6.3 in Chap. 6, it is mentioned that machine learning can be used to detect viruses. The mechanism can be described as follows:

   ① Let computers learn from samples of harmless files and harmful files (supervised learning, classification).
   ② Extract features of harmless files and harmful files respectively and produce the model for identification.
   ③ Use the produced model to identify new files.

   If your answer is "impossible", you can also get scores if you give comprehensible reasons such as viruses may destroy AI first and then AI cannot work.

*2. Generally, if confidentiality and integrity are increased, availability will decrease, and if availability is increased, confidentiality and integrity will decrease. Some details are as follows.

Confidentiality versus availability: Implementing strong encryption and strict access controls can greatly enhance confidentiality. However, this can reduce availability because decryption and access controls may slow down and restrict access to information.

Integrity versus availability: Implementing rigorous integrity checks and validation procedures ensures that data remains accurate and unaltered. However, this can slow down the access process because data changes are closely scrutinized, and suspicious activities may result in access rejection.

*3. See Table 10.12.

Table 10.12 Difference between symmetric key and public key cryptosystems

	Symmetric key cryptosystem	Public key cryptosystem
Key for encryption/decryption	Same	Different
Sending the key in advance	Required	Unnecessary
Mechanism/processing	Easy	Complex
Speed of encryption/decryption	Fast	Slow
Methods of encryption	DES, 3DES, AES	RSA

Printed in the United States
by Baker & Taylor Publisher Services